LITTLE COMPTON
HISTORICAL SOCIETY

Published in the United States by Little Compton Historical Society.

ISBN 97809827069-6-1

First Printing: July 2018

Printed in the United States of America by Sheridan Books, Inc.

Cover art: *Memento Mori* by Molly Luce.

Designed by Shelley Bowen.

Remember Me

A GUIDE TO
LITTLE COMPTON'S
46 HISTORIC
CEMETERIES

Essays by
Marjory Gomez O'Toole
Melinda W. Green
Helen Richmond Webb

Photographs by
Bart Brownell
Letty Champion
Chris O'Toole
Marjory Gomez O'Toole

Thank You Sponsors!

Anonymous

Able Engineering, Inc.

The Acebes Family Charitable Fund

Mr. and Mrs. Nathaniel Atwater

Graeme and Claudia Bell

Booth Bricker Foundation

Sean and Shelley Bowen

Fred and Helen Bridge

Briggs Beach

Reverend and
   Mrs. Robert T. Brooks

Scott and Jill Brown

Bart and Michal Brownell

Dominique Browning

Dianne and Sam Bruce

Elizabeth W. Bullock and
   Stephen M. Jordan

Chris and Suzie Burns

Randy Byers

Kevin and Julie Callaghan

The Carter Family

Compton Clambakes and Catering

Bill and Amy Corbett

Keith Crudgington

Solomon F. Cushman

Mr. & Mrs. Charles Dunn

Nina and Christopher Evison

Janet and Jim Field

Robert and Susan Galford

Robin Gaston

Julie and Teg Gebhard

Haffenreffer Seaconnet Point Fund

Kathy and Jack Haire

Kathryn Hoenig and
    Douglass Maynard

Mark Hough

George F. Kilborn

Albert and Cindy Lees

Sarah and Donald Libbey

Jane Lorch

Mary and Robert Marra

Carol McGee

Mr. and Mrs. Donald McNaughton

J. William Middendorf Jr.

Dora and Trip Millikin

Elizabeth P. Millikin

Kris and John Montgomery

Chuck O'Boyle and Rick Rambuss

Timothy and Janice Olson

Dee Osborn

Timothy and Marjory O'Toole

In Memory of Barbara Jewell Pond

Fulton and Kathryn Pontes

Charles and Marcia Pratt

David and Leslie Puth

Joel and Caroline Reich

Clark Schoettle

In Memory of Philip B. Simonds

Richard and Mary Small

Paul and Mary Suttell

Rush Taggart and Dorothy Bedford

Karen and Jim Tung

David and Ellen Wagner

Gurdon and Kathy Wattles

Lynne and Hunter White

Deborah Wiley

Mr. and Mrs. Alan Willemsen

WELCOME

Welcome to Little Compton and its historic cemeteries! We're so pleased you share our interest in these fascinating and important places, and we hope you find this guidebook helpful.

At the moment, Little Compton has 46 known historic cemeteries, but this number was hard to calculate and is sure to change as we continue to research and explore our community. The Rhode Island Historical Cemetery Commission (rihistoriccemeteries.org) currently lists 50 numbered cemeteries (LC001-LC050) on their excellent website. We subtract two because they are actually in Tiverton (LC001 & LC002); we subtract two more because they are not yet historic (LC014 & LC044 – but we still include them in this guide because they are of interest); we subtract another one because it probably never really existed (LC041); and we add one that we confirmed during the research for this book (LC051).

Forty-six seems like a huge number of cemeteries for one community, but when we realize that Tiverton, our neighbor to the north, has 90, and other Rhode Island communities have 100 or more, it seems rather modest. Colonial Rhode Island followed the practice of using family burying grounds, while nearby Plymouth and Massachusetts used common burying grounds shared by many families. Because Little Compton was originally part of the Plymouth Colony but was settled by many Rhode Island families, we see both customs at work in our community, resulting in many more cemeteries than our Massachusetts neighbors and far fewer than other Rhode Island towns.

This guidebook describes each of Little Compton's historic cemeteries and provides you with some insights into the lives of the people buried there. We have tried to be very clear about which cemeteries are okay to visit and which are not. You are free to visit many of them during daylight hours. Some require an appointment, and we have provided a contact number. Some are not available for visitation. Please be respectful of the visitation policies established by the cemetery owners and neighbors. Some of the cemeteries are privately owned, others are surrounded by private property, and trespassing is a crime.

If you notice something amiss during one of your cemetery visits, please call the Little Compton Historical Society at 401-635-4035. We are keeping track of cemeteries and gravestones in need of repair, and we are making those repairs as quickly as our funding and volunteer resources allow. We are always in need of volunteers and supporters, and we invite you to join us in our efforts to better understand and preserve Little Compton's historic cemeteries.

Sincerely,

Bart Brownell
President, Board of Directors
Little Compton Historical Society

Detail from John Dye's gravestone, 1716, Old Burying Ground on the Commons. Photo by Bart Brownell.

ACKNOWLEDGEMENTS

Putting this guidebook together was a big project, especially for a little historical society. Forty-six cemeteries to research (all the way back to the 1700s), to visit, to talk about with owners and neighbors, to photograph, to write about, to edit, to design pages for, and finally to proofread. We worked right up to the deadline – but we did it – and all with a team of volunteers that would be the envy of any employer.

Our first volunteer started working on this project about 100 years ago. Local historian Benjamin Franklin Wilbour devoted his life to researching and documenting Little Compton history. He transcribed every gravestone in Little Compton, and then years later, he did it all over again to make sure his transcriptions were accurate. His work has been invaluable to us and in many cases is the only record that remains for damaged or missing gravestones.

Our next team of volunteers, Helen and Fred Bridge, worked in the 1990s. After pursuing training in gravestone conservation and preservation, Fred restored a number of cemeteries throughout Little Compton and continues to straighten and repair gravestones today. Helen organized all of the information concerning Little Compton cemeteries into an extremely useful index of every gravestone in Little Compton (available at littlecompton.org) and worked with John Sterling and the Rhode Island Historic Cemetery Commission to add the information to their powerful database (rihistoriccemeteries.org). A decade later, Letty Champion, assisted by Barbara Austin, used their work to find and photograph Little Compton's historic gravestones, an enormous task, and added those images to the database. We referred to both the index and the database hundreds of times during the course of this project and have used many of Letty's photographs in this book.

About six months ago we began researching individual cemeteries for the *Remember Me* project, and we were delighted to have offers of research and writing help from Tom Rice, Helen Richmond Webb, Margaret Webb and Melinda W. Green. Tom worked in the town vault and found some information that existed nowhere else. Helen and Margaret researched and wrote a fascinating essay about the Captain Edward Richmond Lot, the final resting place for their earliest Little Compton ancestors. Melinda researched and wrote about five cemeteries, often spending long hours next to me in the town vault or visiting cemeteries together. I know you will enjoy her engaging essays on the Henry Head Senior Burying Ground, the Stoddard Burying Ground, the Manley Burying Ground, the Brightman Lot and the Perry Simmons Burying Ground. In addition, Melinda read 300-years' worth of Town Council and other records to provide essential information on the Old Burying Ground on the Commons, reinterments, the lost burying ground at Town Farm and local people buried without inscribed gravestones. We are very grateful for their contributions.

Bart Brownell, our Board President, took the lion's share of photographs for this book visiting cemeteries in all kinds of weather and all times of the day to capture just the right shots. Board Member, Fred Bridge assisted by cleaning gravestones before their photo shoots. I think you will agree that Bart's photographs make this guidebook celebratory rather than somber.

Shelley Bowen, another Board Member, took hundreds of pages from our writers and hundreds of images from our photographers and skillfully designed this beautiful volume. Shelley is a professional graphic artist, who volunteers her time and remains cool and calm in the face of my last-minute edits and impossibly tight deadlines. We cannot thank her enough.

Our team of editors and proofreaders are still working tonight as I write this note thanking them. They include Board Members Bart Brownell, Steven Lubar, Caroline Wordell, Carolyn Montgomery, Randy Byers, Fred Bridge and Mike Steers, as well as volunteers Janice Gomez, Roger Guillemette, Melinda Green and Lease Plimpton.

We are also grateful to Professor Jon Marcoux for his ground penetrating radar surveys, Chris O'Toole for designing project logos and contributing photographs, and Dominique Browning for offering her painting by Molly Luce for our cover art.

Finally, I thank the dozens of local property owners who allowed us to explore and research the burying grounds on or near their properties. Everyone was hospitable and helpful, and many served as our personal guides to places we could not have found on our own. The Little Compton Town Council, the Town Clerk's Office, the Tax Assessor's Office and the Town Maintenance Staff have been similarly hospitable and helpful.

Though it was big, this project came together because of a wonderful team of volunteers who approached their multitude of tasks with the same level of skill and dedication they bring/brought to their professional lives. It has been my personal pleasure to work with each of them on *Remember Me*, and it is now my pleasure to share the results of our efforts with you.

Marjory O'Toole

Marjory Gomez O'Toole
Remember Me Project Director
Executive Director, Little Compton Historical Society

TABLE OF CONTENTS

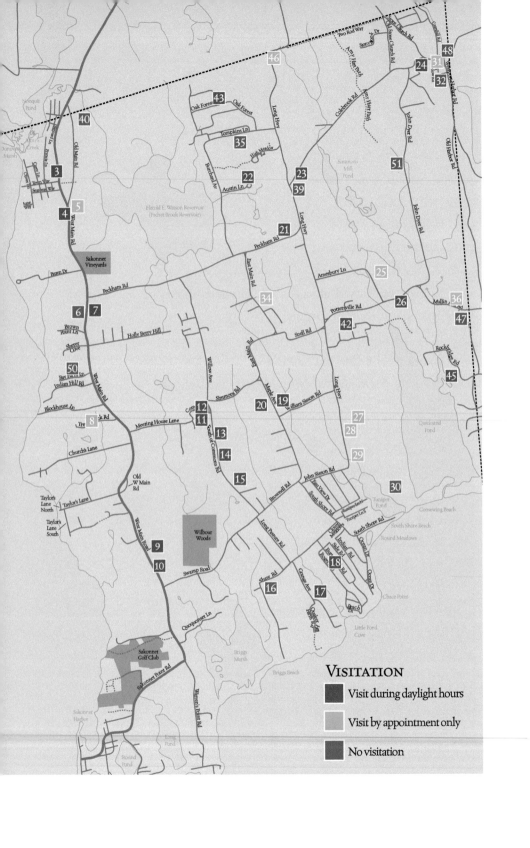

VISITATION

Visit during daylight hours

Visit by appointment only

No visitation

Painting by Molly Luce.

1 & 2

HISTORICAL CEMETERY 1 & 2

Little Compton no longer has a Historical Cemetery 1 or 2 because both were determined to be in Tiverton. Those numbers have been retired. For more information, please go to rihistoriccemeteries.org and search for TV029 and TV030.

Photo by Bart Brownell.

3

ALMY CEMETERY

Near 63 Old Main Road - Windmill Hill
Gravestones dated 1803-Present.
Owned by the Almy heirs.
Visitation during daylight hours.
Roadside parking.

The Almy's homestead farm on Windmill Hill accessed the Great West Road via a long tree-lined path. At its end was the family burying ground with a spectacular view of the Sakonnet River. Today the view is slightly obstructed, and the main road has rerouted around the hill, but the Almy cemetery still stands.

This cemetery is one of the few family burial grounds actively in use in Little Compton today. A large lot with 66 burials, it contains white marble nineteenth-century stones and twentieth-century granite stones, some with names and birth dates carved in advance for people living today.

Though it is possible that there are earlier unmarked graves, the Honorable Sanford Almy, a Revolutionary War Veteran, and his wife Lydia Gray likely established the cemetery in 1803 when they had the sad task of burying their 19-year-old-son John Almy. Sanford and Lydia buried two daughters here as well: Fanny, age two, in 1813 and Lorinda, age 25, in 1822. Sanford reserved the burial place for his family members in his will when he died in 1844, and his descendants continued to "except and reserve" it well into the twentieth century. They also established a perpetual maintenance fund with the Town of Little Compton in the 1950s.

The Almy Cemetery contains a wide mix of surnames including Briggs, Davenport, Davis, Hunt, Jackson, Lawton, Pratt, Snell and Wilcox. All connect to the Almy family through marriage.

A number of veterans are at rest here including the Honorable Sanford Almy who served in the Revolution and his grandson Pardon Almy Jr. who graduated from Harvard University in 1861 and died during the Second Battle of Bull Run in 1862. His body was never recovered, but his family honored him here with a memorial stone.

Perhaps the best-known person who will someday be buried here is Miss Lois Almy. Miss Almy will turn 101 in 2018. She taught Little Compton's first grade students for 31 years and is remembered fondly by hundreds of local residents today.

4
WOODMAN LOT WEST

West side of West Main Road -
   Opposite 120 West Main Road
Gravestones dated 1760-1830.
Owned by the Woodman heirs per
   John Woodman's 1831 will.
This lot appears to have been abandoned by the family.
Roadside parking.

This small lot is in very poor condition, perhaps the worst in Little Compton. It contains finely carved stones from the John Stevens Shop in Newport and the Throop Shop in Bristol, but many are broken, and most lean against the roadside wall.

Photo by Bart Brownell.

The Woodmans owned three 100-acre "Great Lots" along Little Compton's Great West Road. The highway divided their farm in two, east and west. As new generations of sons came of age, their parents gave them portions of the farm. This western portion of the Woodman homestead fell to Sylvester Woodman around the time of his marriage in 1735. Rather than bury his dead in the older family burying ground across the street, Sylvester established his own burying ground on his own property.

His son John (1746-1831) attempted to preserve the lot by writing in his will, "that my family burial place be reserved for sacred purpose, forever, it to be six rods [99 feet] north and south and three rods (49½ feet) east and west." Many local burying grounds began at first without walls and were walled in later by descendants. Stone walls protect cemeteries from harm and signal their existence long after their creation. The Sylvester Woodman lot is not walled in today, and it is possible it never was. It has suffered because of it, and today appears to be only a third of the size John Woodman intended it to be.

Ground penetrating radar (see page 136) done in 2018, located what are likely the now unmarked graves of approximately nine people buried in this lot. With sufficient funds and volunteer labor it will be possible to reinstall some of the gravestones leaning against the wall. Others may be beyond repair.

Photo by Marjory O'Toole.

Photo by Bart Brownell.

5

WOODMAN LOT EAST

120 West Main Road
Gravestones dated 1710-1907.
Owned by the heirs of Humphrey Woodman per his 1868 will.
This burying ground appears to have been abandoned by the family.
Visitation by appointment only.
Contact the Little Compton Historical Society
 401-635-4035 or lchistory@littlecompton.org.
Accessed via private property. Private driveway. Do not block.
Roadside parking.

   This family lot served the Woodman family and later their Peckham in-laws for over 200 years. Lieutenant John Woodman and his wife Hannah Timberlake owned the farm in 1710 when their granddaughter Mary died and was buried here. Mary's gravestones, a headstone and a footstone, were carved by John Stevens and display his hanging-toothed skull design. They bear the oldest date in this burying ground. Other relatives followed, and many have fine gravestones carved by members of the Stevens Shop and John Bull of Newport.

Like many eighteenth-century Little Compton families, the Woodmans were slaveholders. In 1754 Robert Woodman's will shows that three enslaved people lived here; a woman named Prue, a girl named Peg and a boy named Toby. Twenty-six years later Constant Woodman freed Toby in his will and ordered his estate to support him "if he behaves, if he steals or behaves ill to return to bondage." Whether they were enslaved or partially free, as Toby was at the end of his life, the people of color who lived and worked in the Woodman household may be buried here. In 2018 ground penetrating radar revealed what may be unmarked graves near the western wall of this burying ground. The marked family graves are all to the east. To date, no inscribed gravestones for people enslaved in Little Compton are known.

The Woodmans cared deeply about this cemetery and like many residents took pains to protect it. When Humphrey Woodman died in 1868 he divided the farm among his daughters and wrote:

Photo by Bart Brownell.

I do however reserve the burial ground which is on said homestead farm as the same is now walled in, and my will and meaning is that this ground shall be and remain a burial ground or place for all my children and their children when the occasion may require it to the latest generation with liberty to pass & repass to the same without molestation.

He went on to ensure that he would be properly buried and memorialized:

Pay just debts and funeral expenses and I do order my Executor herein after named to cause to be erected at my grave good & substantial gravestones with suitable inscriptions upon the same within one year after my decease.

Humphrey's daughters reasserted their right to the cemetery in a later deed to Peleg Peckham:

> Reserving however the Burying Ground on said premises and a pass to and from the same for the purposes of repair, burial, removal of the dead, or visitation at all times forever, as occasion may arise.

This newer wording reflects a changing attitude among nineteenth-century residents who began to see family burying grounds as old-fashioned places in need of repair and protection, and who contemplated moving (and sometimes did move) the bodies of their loved ones to newer, more fashionable, cemeteries both in and out of town.

6

IRISH LOT

Across the street from the Friends Meeting House, 234 West Main Road.
Two gravestones dated 1707 and 1717.
Owned by the Irish heirs per Samuel Irish's 1816 will.
This lot appears to be abandoned by the family.
Surrounded by private property.
No visitation.
Parking across the road between the street and the stone wall of the Friends Meeting House.
Visible from the roadside.

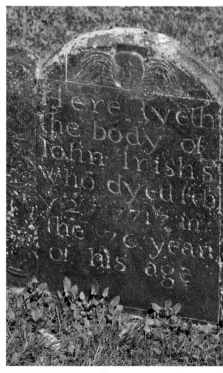

Photo by Bart Brownell.

This small family lot reveals evidence of great change. A variety of historic cemetery surveys indicate that there used to be more stones here. In the 1950s the Town Council directed town workers to go to the lot and do whatever they thought was best. At the time of publication, the single remaining foot-stone sits to the side of its headstone instead of in back of it, facing the wrong direction. These are signs that through the years people

Photo by Bart Brownell.

have reworked this burying ground in ways they thought were appropriate at the time.

New England's eighteenth-century Christians buried their dead laying east to west. Gravestones were always sold in sets of headstones and footstones. Families placed the headstone at the west end of the grave with its inscription facing west and the footstone at the east end of the grave with its inscription facing east. The deceased laid in between the two, as though they were in a small bed, with their heads near the headstone and their feet near the footstone. This particular arrangement faced the departed toward the rising sun, so that on Judgment Day they could quickly rise up and join their Savior. Placing the stones this way also made it possible to visit graves and read inscriptions without stepping on anyone's remains.

The stones here belong to John Irish (1641-1717) and Elizabeth Thurston Irish (c.1654-1707) the first Irish family members to settle in Little Compton. Elizabeth's grave sat for a decade after her death with no inscribed stone, but after John's death in 1717 his heirs purchased two sets of similar stones from the John Stevens Shop in Newport. Both are carved with the pointy-chinned angel design attributed to John Stevens I by gravestone scholar Vincent Luti. Elizabeth's stone is slightly damaged, but John's remains in remarkably good condition. The footstone is John's.

The Irish stones are an excellent reminder that the death date carved into a gravestone is not necessarily the date the stone was carved. Many Little Compton gravestones are backdated with the person's date of death but were actually carved several years, sometimes many years, after a person's death in the carving style that was popular at that particular time.

Like so many early English families, the Irishes stayed in Little Compton for generations, expanding their farm when the opportunity arose and then dividing it among their sons. Early generations were Quakers and may be buried in the cemetery behind the Friends Meeting House across the street. John Irish's second wife Priscilla Southworth Talbot Irish (b. 1645) has no surviving inscribed stone, so we do not know her burial place nor her exact death date. We do know her estate went through probate in 1722 and can assume that to be her year of death. Later generations of Irishes chose to be buried in the Old Burying Ground on the Commons.

In 1816 John and Elizabeth's grandson Samuel (1742-1816) reserved the burying ground for his family forever.

> My will is and I do order that the Family burying ground in the North East Corner of my North East Meadow be and remain a burying place for ever and not be sold but remain for the use of my near relatives to be buried therein.

But it was John and Elizabeth's son John (1699-1773), Samuel's father, whose last will and testament hopefully had the greatest impact on the Irish family:

> Exhorting my children to live in Love one with another as ye God of Love & Peace may bless them.

The Irish family name has died out among Little Compton residents, but a surprising number of Irish descendants come to Little Compton each year to learn more about their ancestors and pay their respects at John's and Elizabeth's graves.

Photo by Bart Brownell.

7

FRIENDS BURYING GROUND

234 West Main Road, in back of the Friends Meeting House
Gravestones dated 1714-1903, numerous fieldstones and unmarked graves.
Owned by the Little Compton Historical Society.
Visitation during daylight hours unless a private event is taking place.
Park on the lawn between the road and the stone wall.

Quakers were among Little Compton's earliest English settlers, arriving in the last quarter of the seventeenth century. Some, like the Rouses, who operated a tavern next door to the Meeting House, had witnessed great persecution in other parts of the Colonies. Even in Little Compton they were subject to Quaker censuses ordered by Massachusetts colonial officials. The "List of people called Quakers" in 1732 and 1733 included David Irish, Thomas Brownell, John Wilbour, William Wilbour, Samuel Wilbour, John Taylor, Jonathan Thurston, John Taylor Junior and Mary Peckham.

The Friends built a meeting house on this site in 1700. It was Little Compton's first building dedicated solely to religious purposes. It was damaged by the Great Gale of 1815, and the Friends recycled its materials to build the structure that stands today.

Though some Quakers, like Samuel and Mary Wilbor (who lived in what is now the Wilbor House Museum), created family burying grounds on their own farms, many others chose to be buried here. Throughout the eighteenth century, Little Compton's Quakers used simple fieldstone markers with no inscriptions. There were two exceptions.

Elizabeth Peckham Taylor, the wife of Peter Taylor, was buried here in 1714 and has John Stevens gravestones decorated with his hanging-toothed skull design. Susanna Wilbor, the wife of Thomas Wilbor, died in 1729 at the age of 26 and she, too, has an inscribed stone. Hers is a plain style offered by the Stevens Shop, with lettering but no decorations.

In the early-eighteenth century New England Friends experienced a tightening of their behavioral codes, like the need for plainness in all things. So while it was acceptable at the time of Elizabeth's death to have an image on her gravestones, Susanna's family made a simpler choice with only lettering, and the Friends who followed them chose even more simply using only plain fieldstones as grave markers until the very end of the century.

As the nineteenth century approached, plain white marble stones with simple inscriptions became popular. Ruth Wood's is the earliest, dated 1793. Many of these stones display the Friends' plain speech using phrases like "second month" and "sixth day" instead of the typical names of the months and days. This was done to avoid honoring the Greek and Roman gods for whom the months and days are named.

The gravestone of Edward W. Howland (1833-1903), Little Compton's "Last Quaker," is here, as is the stone of his grandmother, Innocent Howland (1778-1856), known in local histo-ries as "The Beautiful Quakeress." Edward's aunt Mehitable Hicks Howland (1813-1875) has a stone here and a second stone in the Seaconnet Cemetery. See more of her story on page 21.

In the spring of 2018 ground penetrating radar (see page 136) indicated that there are dozens of unmarked graves in the Friends Burying Ground to the east of the marked graves. It is possible that the fieldstone markers for these graves have been lost through the years. It is also possible they were never marked.

Ground penetrating radar reveals unmarked graves. Image by Professor Jon Marcoux.

8

CAPT. EDWARD RICHMOND LOT

Treaty Rock Road
Gravestones dated 1696-1845 and uninscribed stones.
Visitation by appointment only.
Contact the Little Compton Historical Society 401-635-4035 or
  lchistory@littlecompton.org

In an 1868 deed the burial ground at Treaty Rock Farm was described as "being rectangular & 28 feet East and West and 46 feet North and South." When agricultural improvements were made in 2005 a 30-foot protective area outside the current fence was required by the USDA Natural Resources Conservation Service because of the possibility of unmarked graves of slaves, servants or Native Americans. Today the fenced area, containing all known graves, is approximately the same in east to west dimension as in the old deed, but smaller north to south, with the additional area most

Photo by Bart Brownell.

likely having been to the north. There are 19 marked graves, 14 of which are identified. All but one are members of the Richmond family.

The markers range from large, horizontal, uninscribed fieldstone ledger, or "wolf," stones more typical of seventeenth-century burials, to carved slate and marble. Most have both head and footstones. Five stones have identified carvers. The oldest is that of Captain Edward Richmond, one of the Sakonnet Proprietors and the first English settler of the property. His grave is marked with both plain ledgers and upright stones by John Stevens I, which would have been carved several years after Edward's death in 1696 as Stevens did not arrive in Little Compton until 1700. The headstone of his grandson Judge William Richmond (1694-1770) is an unusual portrait stone by John Stevens III. Other gravestones are attributed to William Throop and Thomas Diman.

Most of the identified graves are from 1769 to 1817, as this was the primary cemetery for the male heirs of Judge William. All but one of his sons are buried here as well as their spouses, some of their children, an unmarried granddaughter and an infant great-great granddaughter. The only person in the graveyard not a member of the Richmond family — perhaps a household servant — Sarah Sanford (1760-1778) was from Portsmouth, Rhode Island. She died during the British occupation of Aquidneck Island, which is a possible explanation for her burial in Little Compton. Her grave is marked with a ledger as well as a carved headstone. It is reasonable to presume her family arranged for the inscribed marker after the British occupation ended in 1779.

Two of the unidentified graves are marked only with uninscribed ledger stones. Captain Edward outlived two wives, Abigail Davis and Amy Bull. One might speculate that these are their graves. Three graves have broken markers—granite head and foot stones—and no information has been found.

A succession of Williams owned the farm until the mid-twentieth century. Judge William left the farm to his son, Colonel William (1727-1807), who lived there until his death and is buried in the cemetery. Colonel William and his wife Hannah Gray had no children, so he left the property to his nephew William (1770-1850), who fashioned himself William II. He was born in Dighton and later moved to Providence. William II started his career as a mariner and became a shipowner, merchant, businessman and public official. His maritime interests provide a plausible explanation for several memorial stones in the cemetery. His two brothers died in Havana, Cuba within a year of each other, and his first cousin Charles died in a shipwreck off the coast of Sweden in October of 1803, only six months later.

While William II did not reside in Little Compton, the family visited often. William and his second wife, Lydia Brownell were married in town, and the latest identified grave is that of baby Mary, granddaughter of William II, who died in 1845 while her family was visiting from Yonkers, New York. In 1851 his second son, James Cook wrote in the preface to his epic poem about Metacomet:

> In the south part of Rhode Island there is an estate which was never owned by any body but Indians and Richmonds. It is yet a part of my father's estate; and it will be the last portion which shall be rent from the hands of his children. In that dear home of our fathers, I used, in my childhood, to seat myself upon Treaty Rock, where Col. Church, in the life time of Edward Richmond, made that alliance with Awashonks, the Queen-Sachem of the Seconet Indians, which broke the heart of Metacomet.

Despite James Cook Richmond's sentiments, after the death of William II in 1850, his heirs sold the farm in portions over the next 18 years to William H. Chase, who farmed the property for several decades and owned it outright between 1868 and 1899. The various deeds prescribed that the burial ground remain the property of the Richmond heirs. After James Cook's son William purchased the farm back from Chase in 1899, he gradually acquired the rights to the burial ground from various descendants.

He left the farm and the burial ground to his son, the last William, who did not have children. The property was deeded to a distant Richmond cousin and remains in the family.

Judge William Richmond's Portrait Stone. Photo by Bart Brownell.

Photo by Bart Brownell.

9

OLD WILBOR BURYING GROUND

548 West Main Road
Gravestones dated 1827-1928 and numerous fieldstones.
Owned by the heirs of Samuel Wilbor per his 1740 will.
Visitation during daylight hours.
Park at the Little Compton Historical Society, Wilbor House Museum.
There is no charge to visit the cemetery.
Visitors are asked to check in with the receptionist when
  the Historical Society is open.
Walk east to the end of the Historical Society's property (just before the
  ground gets rough). Then turn south (to the right) and walk through
  the gate. The cemetery is directly ahead.
Access is slightly challenging requiring about a four-minute walk over
  uneven ground.

Samuel and Mary (Potter) Wilbor came to Little Compton around 1690 from Portsmouth, Rhode Island. Their descendants occupied the family farm until 1920, and their home survives today as the Little Compton Historical Society's Wilbor House Museum. Three of Samuel's brothers established similar farms in other parts of town, and two of their burying grounds survive. (See pages 45 & 75.)

Samuel Wilbor designated this plot as a permanent family cemetery when he wrote his will in 1730 a decade before his death. Mary and their son Thomas were very likely already buried here because Samuel does not mention them in his will. Samuel wrote that the burying ground should, "Remain for that use and for no other forever never to be sold nor put away that so my family have liberty to bury in it." He was one of the first Little Compton property owners to permanently exclude his family burying ground from future sales of the farm and to ensure his family could use the cemetery forever. His descendants did use it, for the next 200 years.

The original Samuel and Mary Wilbor farm was about 120 acres and stretched from West Main Road to South of Commons Road. Each new generation of Samuel and Mary's descendants acquired more land in the neighborhood and distributed it to their sons. Eventually, the extended family owned almost all the land on both sides of West Main Road from Taylor's Lane to south of Swamp Road including Wilbour's Woods. (The spelling of Wilbor varies.) This burying ground served many generations of this large branch of the Wilbor family.

Samuel and a number of other early Wilbors were Quakers. Like many eighteenth-century Little Compton residents of various faiths, they chose to use uninscribed fieldstones as their headstones and footstones until the nineteenth century.

Old Wilbor Burying Ground prior to repairs. LCHS Collection.

The Old Wilbor Burying Ground is particularly interesting, not only because of the people buried here but because of the people removed from here. After the creation of the nearby Seaconnet Cemetery in 1880 (see page 19), a number of Wilbor relatives petitioned the Town Council to remove their loved ones from this old family lot and move them to other more fashionable or convenient cemeteries.

> 1899   *Isaac & Horatio Wilbur petition to remove the bodies of their deceased friends from the Wilbor Cemetery to the "New Yard" or Seaconnet Cemetery. This request likely included the remains of Governor Isaac C. Wilbour who died in 1837. Governor Wilbour held many political offices including Governor of Rhode Island from 1806 to 1807 and United States Congressman from 1807 to 1809.*

> 1899   *The children of Benjamin and Abigail Wilbour asked to move their parents' remains to the Seaconnet Cemetery.*

> 1909   *Lizzie Gray moved her father George A. Gray (his mother was Judith Wilbor) to Swan Point Cemetery in Providence.*

> 1909   *Noah Hervey Wilbor of Acushnet moved his parents Peleg and Elizabeth Wilbor to the Seaconnet Cemetery.*

> 1918   *Oliver H. Wilbor was moved to the family plot in the Old Burying Ground on the Commons. His wife Abby H., the last Wilbor to live in the Wilbor House, was moved there as well.*

The Old Wilbor Burying Ground was in severe disarray in the 1960s. Carlton Brownell of the Little Compton Historical Society oversaw its repair and recruited his high school students to provide the labor. Note that some of the stones near the west wall break the tradition of inscriptions facing west. The Wilbor family may have made this decision because the stones were so close to the

Old Wilbor Burying Ground after repairs. LCHS Collection.

wall, or the restorers may have decided to face them this way to make them easier to read.

Notable Gravestones

Baby. In the 1800s inscribed gravestones for unnamed babies became more common.

Abby Catharine Gray Wilbour was a midwife and an active suffragist.

10

SEACONNET CEMETERY

Also known as The New Wilbour Cemetery
Near 566 West Main Road
Gravestones dated 1832-2008.
Owned by the Seaconnet Cemetery Company.
Visitation during daylight hours.
Roadside parking.

The stories associated with the founding of this cemetery in 1880 have reached legendary proportions.

The real truth may never be determined, but the story goes like this…

Isaac C. Wilbour, a man known for naming the Rhode Island Red chicken and running the largest poultry farm in the world, wanted to establish a new modern cemetery, like the Union Cemetery, for his family and friends. He chose the former site of Oliver Wilbor's windmill on the east side of West Main Road just a little south of Oliver's house, now the Wilbor House Museum.

Isaac and his neighbor George Gray had been arguing bitterly over which of them owned the real Betty Alden House (Isaac did.), and George was holding a grudge. George owned a cottage next to the proposed cemetery and went to the Rhode Island General Assembly to pass a new law stating no new cemeteries could be created that close to a house.

Isaac read about the new law in the newspaper one evening. It would go into effect at midnight, ruining his plans. Isaac flew into action and consulted with Charles Wilbour Howland who shared his interest in creating a new cemetery. They had to find a way to establish the cemetery

Photo by Bart Brownell.

before midnight, and that meant burying someone there right away, but there was no one waiting for burial. Charles came up with a solution. He offered to have his wife Mehitable Hicks Howland's remains removed from her 1875 grave at the Friend's Meeting House and reinterred in the new cemetery. Isaac ordered it done, and so it was, with the last shovelful of dirt tossed by lantern light but safely before midnight. Even today some people question whether Mehitable was really moved or if the digging of the new grave was just for show. However, ground penetrating radar performed at the Little Compton Friends Burying Ground in 2018 showed disturbed earth near Mehitable's gravestone without the strong reflection signals at a depth of six feet that was seen for other nearby graves. This is evidence that Mehitable's first grave in the Friend's Burying Ground may indeed be empty.

With George Gray defeated, the Seaconnet Cemetery Company formed and began selling cemetery lots by deeds registered by the Town Clerk. The earliest are dated August 1880 and the latest, to Theodora Wilbour Peckham, is 1958. Beginning in 1880 the Town Council received and approved several requests to move Wilbour family members from the Old Wilbor Burying Ground to the north to the new family cemetery. (There are multiple spellings of Wilbor.)

In 1885 Charles Edwin Wilbour, America's first Egyptologist, and his wife Charlotte Beebe, an active suffragist, buried their 20-year-old daughter Zoe in the Seaconnet Cemetery after she suffered a long illness. The Wilbours were devastated by this loss and decided to build a bell tower in Zoe's honor similar to the ones they had seen during their tours of Europe. The tower has memorial stones inside it for many of their ancestors. Eventually Zoe's parents were also buried here. In 1937 the Wilbour's older daughter Theodora removed the remains of Zoe and her parents and had them moved to Woodlawn cemetery in New York. Later that year she ordered the

Seaconnet Cemetery shortly after it opened. LCHS Collection.

demolition of her family home Awashonks once located at the corner of West Main Road and Swamp Road. The Little Compton Historical Society preserves many family items removed from the house by twenty-year-old Carlton Brownell with Theodora's permission.

Notable Gravestones

Governor Isaac Wilbour (1763-1837) held many political offices including Governor of Rhode Island from 1806 to 1807 and United States Congressman from 1807 to 1809.

Sarah Soule Wilbour (1804-1891) was a prolific local historian and an activist who worked for abolition and women's suffrage. She was the daughter of Governor Isaac Wilbour and the mother of Charles Edwin Wilbour. As a widow, unable to vote, she refused to pay her taxes because it was taxation without representation. She offered instead to pay for civic improvement projects. Shortly before her death she raised funds for the monument to Elizabeth Alden Pabodie in the Old Burying Ground on the Commons.

David Patten (1888-1975) was a *Providence Journal* editor who wrote frequently about his Little Compton boyhood in his columns and published two books of local history and personal memories entitled *Three Sides to the Sea* and *Adventures in a Remembered World.*

Benjamin Franklin Wilbour Jr. (1887-1964) dedicated much of his adult life to researching and recording the history of Little Compton. His masterwork is an 800-page town-wide genealogy entitled *Little Compton Families.* Much of the work of the Little Compton Historical Society today begins with the work of B.F. Wilbour.

Photo by Bart Brownell.

Photo by Bart Brownell.

11

UNION CEMETERY

The Commons
Gravestones dated 1802-Present.
Owned by the Union Cemetery Society.
Visitation during daylight hours.
Park on the Commons.
This is an active cemetery. For information contact William Richmond
  508-397-1704 or billrichmond@cox.net.

The Union Cemetery is Little Compton's first modern cemetery reflecting changes in burial practices that took place in parts of Europe and America during Victorian times.

Four town fathers, John Church, Isaac B. Richmond, Jonathan Brownell and Benjamin Seabury formed a not-for-profit society and established the Union Cemetery to the south of the Commons in 1855. They were dissatisfied with the care given to the Old Burying Ground on the Commons by the town. At that time the town's common burial ground allowed all town residents and any "strangers" who died while they were here to be buried on the Commons without paying for a lot. Families who could afford it would pay for a coffin, grave digging and in some cases gravestones. Paupers were buried at town expense with fieldstone markers or perhaps no markers at all. Maintenance on the Old Burying Ground was minimal. Once or twice a year someone would scythe the hay that grew among the stones, and every twenty years or so, the town would pay someone to fill in sunken graves and straighten toppled stones.

The founders of the Union Cemetery Society envisioned something very different. Inspired by the "garden cemetery" movement of the early 1800s, they planned an orderly, professionally-designed cemetery, rather than a simple burying ground. It was to have clearly defined lots sold and deeded to purchasers, specific pathways, curbs, and an elegant wrought iron fence surrounding it. Gravestones were no longer oriented just to the east and west but were erected in various directions, so they were easily readable from the pathways. The cemetery's most expensive lots were in the center of the rectangular space at a crossway, and the less-expensive, smaller lots were located along its edges. The lots sold quickly. Some families purchased

New section.

more than one, so their family members could be buried here for many years. The cemetery's trustees encouraged the creation of perpetual care funds to ensure the manicured look of the cemetery forever.

In 1952 the Union Cemetery needed additional space and expanded to the south under the direction of its steward of over 50 years, Carlton Brownell. Gravestones are allowed along its edges while flat stones are used in the center to encourage the open, park-like atmosphere favored by many cemeteries today.

Notable Gravestones – Original Section

Colonel Henry T. Sisson (1831-1910) is honored with this statue for his daring 1863 rescue of the Massachusetts 44th Regiment (1,100 men) under siege by Confederate soldiers at Little Washington, North Carolina. Henry commanded a troop of volunteers on a steamship, under cover of darkness, through Confederate batteries, and despite heavy fire reached the Union forces and broke the siege. The grateful state of Massachusetts commissioned this statue created by Henri Schonhardt and cast by the Gorham Manufacturing Company in Providence. Future Governor of Massachusetts and later President of the United States, Calvin Coolidge was the guest of honor at the statue's elaborate 1917 unveiling ceremonies.

Colonel Henry T. Sisson and Lemuel Sisson.

Lemuel Sisson (1769-1849) brought the Methodist religion and his large family to Little Compton in 1815.

Edith Russell Church Burchard (1868-1942) inherited a fortune from her father, John Church a sheet music publisher, when she was just 19-years old. Edith was the pinnacle of Little Compton society. Her home, Old Acre on the corner of West Main Road and Meeting House Lane, was the most modernly equipped house in town, and her 1897 wedding was the social event of the decade; she sent 1,700 eagerly-received invitations. Around the time of Edith's death and burial, her children moved their father Roswell Burchard's remains here from his original burial at Old Acre.

Edith Russell Church Burchard.

Notable Gravestones – New Section

Robert "Bobby" Whitmarsh (1962-1969) died at the age of seven after a long struggle with cancer. Local artist Betts Woodhouse invited Bobby's mother, Dougie Whitmarsh, to assist with the creation of the bronze sculpture that adorns his stone as a healing way to mourn her loss. His memorial stone is on the eastern edge of the cemetery.

Bobby Whitmarsh.

Carlton Brownell (1917-2013) designed and oversaw the construction of his own memorial at the rear of the cemetery. Carlton is remembered by his nieces and nephews as well as by the people of Little Compton for his seventy years of public service to the community. He was a veteran of two wars, a history teacher at Tiverton High School and worked tirelessly for many local organizations including the Little Compton Historical Society, the Brownell Library and the Union Cemetery.

Carlton Brownell.

Photo by Bart Brownell.

12

OLD BURYING GROUND

The Commons
Gravestones dated 1698-2000 and numerous fieldstones.
Owned by the Town of Little Compton.
Visitation during daylight hours.
Roadside parking.

Little Compton's Old Burying Ground on the Commons is a quintes-sential New England graveyard. Its 1000+ gravestones have attracted tourists since the Civil War. Today almost 350 years after its founding, the Old Burying Ground feels like a place where time stands still, but this manicured space is very different from the seldom-mowed field that served as the town's common burying ground well into the twentieth century.

Little Compton's First Proprietors established this burying ground as one of their first orders of business in Duxbury, Massachusetts in 1677, even before they settled here. Little Compton was established by Plymouth Colony in 1675, absorbed by Massachusetts Bay Colony in 1690, and given to Rhode Island in 1747. As a border town settled by residents of Plymouth and Rhode Island, Little Compton followed both the Plymouth and Massachusetts custom of a common burying ground as well as the Rhode Island practice of individual family cemeteries.

The Old Burying Ground was available at no charge to any town resident or anyone who died while visiting. For its first 125 years the Old Burying Ground operated as intended with no record of maintenance or repair by either the town or the nearby Congregational Church. It was unwalled and mowed, by hand, probably not more than once or twice per year. Families selected specific areas for their burials, though there were no clearly defined family plots.

When the need arose, families hired a gravedigger, often a man of color, to dig a grave for the departed. Funerals were scheduled a day or two after a death. On the day of the funeral mourners gathered at the deceased's home to pray with the family. They carried the coffin by hand or wagon directly to the burying ground and said a few more prayers, then returned to the deceased's home for food and sugared rum. Church services were rare until the late-nineteenth century. The first carved gravestones appeared after 1700. For many years, the majority of graves were marked by fieldstones.

Beginning in 1804, town and church records show that residents began to pay much more attention to the Burying Ground on the Commons:

1787-1821	Church histories report that congregants stroll in the burying ground in between Reverend Mase Shepherd's morning and afternoon church services.
1804	The Town Council grants the United Congregational Society permission to fence in and oversee the care of the Burying Ground while retaining the right to bury residents of Little Compton and "strangers who may die in" the town.
1804-1844	The United Congregational Society maintains and improves the Burying Ground.
1830	The United Congregational Society enlarges the Burying Ground and replaces wooden fences with stone walls.
1843	The Town Council votes to level and repair the public burial ground on the Common at the expense of the town. Three weeks later, the vote is repealed.
1844	Voters at a Town Meeting decide not to purchase a hearse for the town and instead pay the Hearse Association $1 per use of their vehicle for town-funded funerals.
1857	The Town Council takes over the care of the Burying Ground.
1860	Voters approve the expansion of the Burying Ground on the Common. Eleven days later the motion is repealed. Workers rebuild the dismantled stone walls in their original locations.
1870	The Town Council institutes regular yearly (or twice-yearly) mowing of the Burying Ground which continues into the twentieth century.
1870	The Town Council votes to reposition the west end of the Burying Ground wall to include the Negro Burying Ground. This is the first and only mention of a Negro Burying Ground in Little Compton records.
1876	A plan to move the footstones in the Old Burying Ground is indefinitely postponed, yet they were moved at one point. Today all the footstones for children's graves have been

repositioned to be in line with the footstones for adult graves, and there are no longer any footstones for graves marked only with fieldstones.

1876   The Town Council appoints a committee to purchase a new hearse for the use of the town.

1877   One of abutter Henry Brown's fence posts is found set in a grave. The Town prohibits Brown from enclosing part of the Burying Ground and using it as a barnyard for his poultry and other animals.

1877   The Hearse Committee reports that they have purchased a hearse from George F. Brownell of New Bedford for $375. A hearse house is built later that year for about $200.

1885   Town Meeting attendees vote to sell the town hearse. The hearse house is rented out but continues to contain a cell for prisoners. The purchaser of the hearse is supposed to have used it to deliver feed to his chickens.

1899-1918   At least three families petition the Town to move the remains of family members from the Old Burying Ground to other locations, and one family moves remains from a family cemetery into the Old Burying Ground. Similar petitions to remove remains from other town cemeteries are made during this time.

1902   The Town pays workmen to fill sunken graves in the Old Cemetery and straighten headstones.

1914   It takes two men working six days each to mow the Old Cemetery.

1926   The Town Council votes "that complaint having been made that the school children at the Commons have thrown stones at the gravestones and eaten their lunches and scattered the refuse over the graves in the Old Cemetery on the Commons, that the Clerk be instructed to write to James Coombs, Superintendent of Schools and request that he take such steps as may be necessary to prevent the repetition or continuance of the acts complained of."

1930	The Town Council votes to move the hearse house to a point northwest of the Odd Fellows Hall. Today the building is a garage for town maintenance equipment.
1936	The Town Council votes that the burial expenses of any person whom it may be necessary to bury at the expense of the town shall not exceed the sum of $60.
1941	The Town Clerk notes the various cemetery funds established by this time: Briggs Fund $245.43, Jennie Brown $18, Walter Wilbour $32, William Palmer $11; Eliza Palmer $10, John Brown $20, Simeon Bailey $3, Susan Brownell $7, Lenorae Bailey $5, Lois Brown $8, Pardon Brownell $10, Emile Butler $8, Florence G. Wilbour $10.
1943	The Town Council votes that the John Stevens Shop, Newport, be employed to recut the inscriptions on the Tombs of Colonel Benjamin Church and Alice Church, his wife, during the spring and/or summer of 1944, at a cost not to exceed $85. The Little Compton Historical Society shares the expense.
1945-1948	The town is in need of additional cemeteries. The Town Council appoints two committees to "investigate and ascertain if a suitable piece of land can be acquired for cemetery purposes." The second committee recommends three possible properties, but the town makes no purchases.
1946	Voters approve a motion to "dedicate the land on which the Methodist Church now stands as a memorial to those from Little Compton who have served their country in war, to be kept forever open as hallowed ground," and appoint a Memorial Committee to carry out the plan
1950-1951	Voters approve expenses to enclose the west end of the Old Town Cemetery. This area is used for war memorials.
1954	With Town approval, the United Congregational Church funds the installation of the Methodist Bell on "the terrace at the west end of the Old Burying Ground."
1963	The Town pays to reset fallen headstones in the Old Burying Ground.

Slave Row, Old Burying Ground on the Commons. Photo by Chris O'Toole.

Negro Burying Ground

We were unaware of a distinct Negro Burying Ground in Little Compton until Historical Society volunteer Melinda Green completed the herculean effort of reading every Town Council record from the 1700s to the 1970s in the spring of 2018. She found a single reference to the Negro Burying Ground that confirmed its existence, its location and, ultimately, its disappearance.

In 1870, the Little Compton Town Council voted to reposition the west wall surrounding the burying ground on the Commons to include "the Negro Burying Ground." This tells us that prior to 1870 there were separate burying grounds on the Commons, one for white residents adjacent to the Congregational Church that was surrounded by a wall and one to the west for "Negro" residents, enslaved or free, that seems to have been unwalled.

The existence of a Negro Burying Ground on the Commons did not survive in any of our local histories. Instead we read about "Slave Row," a single row of six, nineteenth-century, white marble gravestones belonging to people of color, all of whom were free at the time of their deaths. At least 200 people were enslaved in Little Compton from 1674 to 1816. There were dozens more free people of color living here during that same time period. It is reasonable to assume that a significant number of people of color were buried in the Negro Burying Ground from the 1670s to the 1870s, but

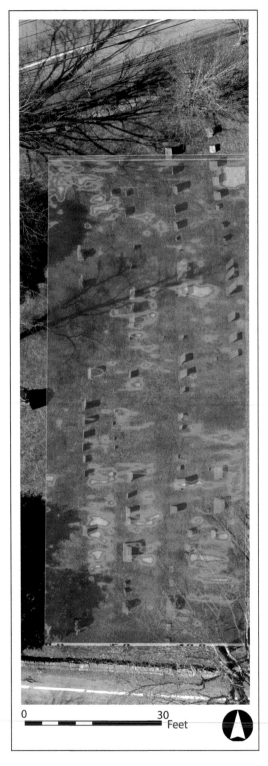

0   30
Feet

there are no surviving gravestones, either inscribed or uninscribed, to mark their graves except for the six marble stones in Slave Row.

Today, because of the relocation of the west wall in 1870 and additional alterations to the wall in the 1950s to accommodate war memorials, all physical evidence of the Negro Burying Ground is gone except for Slave Row, which now looks like the first row in the Old Burying Ground on the Commons. Ground penetrating radar performed by Professor Jon Marcoux of Salve Regina revealed a number of unmarked graves near Slave Row. These may be the graves of additional enslaved or free people of color. There are post-1870 gravestones for white people on three sides of Slave Row. It is possible that these graves encroached on older graves for people of color.

The Little Compton Historical Society recently installed a memorial in Slave Row remembering the more than 200 men, women and children enslaved in Little Compton.

Negro Burying Ground portion of the Old Burying Ground on the Commons showing unmarked graves. Image by Professor Jon Marcoux, Salve Regina University.

Finding Your Way

The map on the following pages will direct you to some of the more notable gravestones in the Old Burying Ground on the Commons.

Every inscribed stone in the burying ground has a Row Number and a Stone Number using a system developed by volunteers Helen Bridge and John Sterling in the 1990s. The numbers for notable gravestones are listed on pages 37–44 The numbers for every inscribed gravestone are available on the Little Compton Historical Society's website (littlecompton.org) under "Historical Resources."

- The left-hand side of the map shows the name on the first gravestone in each row in the burying ground. These gravestones are on the north side of the cemetery – the side closest to Town Hall.
- Use the names to find a specific Row Number.
- Then use the Stone Number to count over to the stone you are seeking, moving north to south – left to right if you are facing the Congregational Church.
- Do not count uninscribed stones.
- Ignore rows of footstones.

For example, if you are looking for Elizabeth Palmer's gravestone, it is Row 28, Stone 9. To find it, walk along the north side of the burying ground until you find the name "Crowley" on the first gravestone in a row. Crowley = Row 28. It is best to walk from the west to the east (from the Methodist Church Bell toward the United Congregational Church) because the names on the stones face that way. Then count over 9 inscribed stones in Row 28 to find Elizabeth's stone.

Old Burying Ground on the Commons

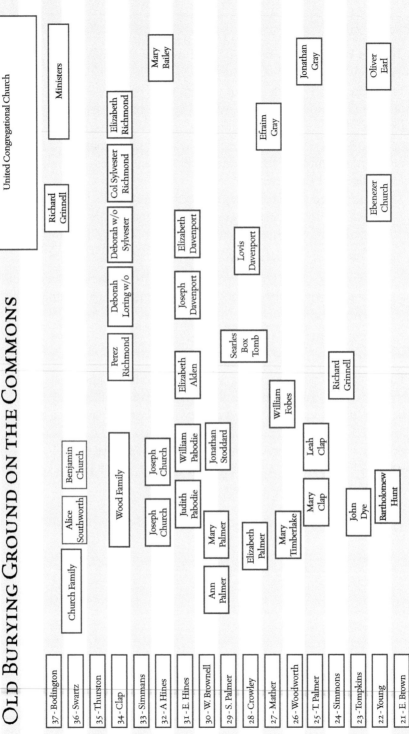

United Congregational Church

Ministers

Richard Grinnell

Mary Bailey

Elizabeth Richmond

Col Sylvester Richmond

Deborah w/o Sylvester

Jonathan Gray

Deborah Loring w/o

Perez Richmond

Elizabeth Davenport

Joseph Davenport

Efraim Gray

Lovis Davenport

Oliver Earl

Ebenezer Church

Searles Box Tomb

Elizabeth Alden

Benjamin Church

Alice Southworth

Church Family

Wood Family

Joseph Church

Joseph Church

William Pabodie

Jonathan Stoddard

William Fobes

Richard Grinnell

Judith Pabodie

Mary Palmer

Leah Clap

Ann Palmer

Elizabeth Palmer

Mary Timberlake

Mary Clap

John Dye

Bartholomew Hunt

37 - Bodington
36 - Swartz
35 - Thurston
34 - Clap
33 - Simmans
32 - A Hines
31 - E. Hines
30 - W. Brownell
29 - S. Palmer
28 - Crowley
27 - Mather
26 - Woodworth
25 - T Palmer
24 - Simmons
23 - Tompkins
22 - Young
21 - E. Brown

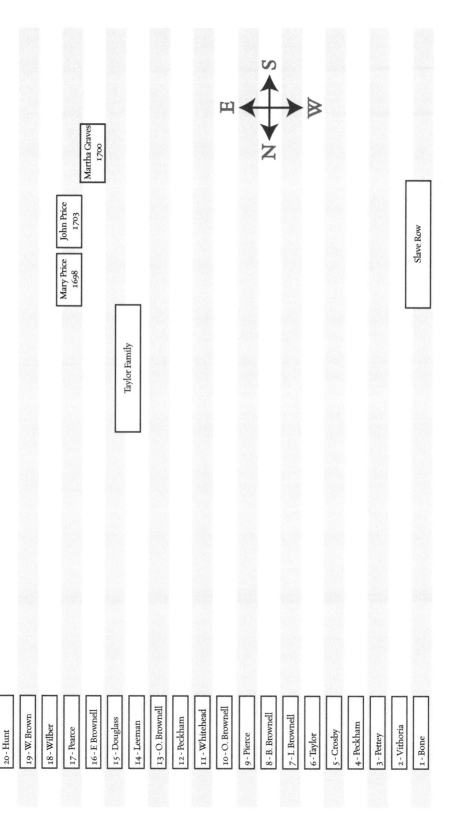

Individual Gravestones in Slave Row. Photos by Chris O'Toole.

Notable Gravestones

Row 1   Slave Row
Memorial to the Enslaved People of Little Compton

The Little Compton Historical Society commissioned this memorial stone in 2016 to mark the 200th anniversary of the end of slavery in Little Compton. Kate Hilliard, the last person to be enslaved in Little Compton, became free on August 5, 1816 as directed in her owner's will. Kate is likely buried nearby without an inscribed gravestone.

Row 1 Stone 4   Lucy Gray

Lucy Gray was enslaved by Pardon Gray in Tiverton but was free by the time of his death in 1814. In 1846 she was living in Little Compton where she contracted with Beniah Borden, the head of a white family, to care for her in her old age in exchange for $1,000.

Row 1 Stone 5   Jane Burgess

Jane Burgess was a free person of color for her entire life. She does not appear in any town records, but her gravestone, now badly weathered, preserved part of her life story.

> *Born in this town March 8, 1788, died Aug 13, 1856 at the residence of the late Dr. West in Tiverton where she lived 40 years in the faithful discharge of her duties.*

Row 1 Stone 6   Primas Collins

Primas Collins was enslaved in the household of Governor John Collins in Newport. The Governor freed Primas when he was four-years old, and the young boy came to Little Compton as the indentured servant of Colonel William Richmond. As a free man Primas slowly acquired property. At the end of his life he owned a 40-acre farm on Meeting House Lane. He married Elisabeth Collins and was the father of two daughters, including Lucy Collins who is buried here. According to local tradition, Primus was elected the "Negro Governor" of Rhode Island, an honorary position.

Row 1 Stone 7   Elisabeth Collins

Elisabeth Collins was the daughter of Sarah Thomas. Her freedom status as a young child is unknown, but she was free as an adult. She married Primas Collins, and together they raised two daughters on their farm on Meeting House Lane.

Row 1 Stone 8   Lucy Collins

Lucy Collins, the daughter of Primas and Elisabeth Collins, lived her whole life as a free woman of color in Little Compton. She inherited her parents' farm on Meeting House Lane and contracted with the Nicholson family to care for her in her old age in exchange for the farm.

Row 1 Stone 9   Sabina G. Lawton

Sabina Gray Lawton was Elisabeth Collins' step-sister. She was the daughter of Fortune and Katherine Gray of Tiverton and later Little Compton. Free from birth, Sabina and her sister Mahala were the first female African American landowners in Little Compton. Sabina married William Wilson Lawton in Newport and raised their sons there. In her old age, Sabina moved back to Little Compton to live with her step-niece Lucy Collins and earned a living by knitting.

Row 2 Stone 1   Frangica Dos Santos Vithoria

Frangica Dos Santos Vithoria was an early Portuguese immigrant from Flores, one of the Azorean Islands. The "W.I." carved on his gravestone stands for Western Islands, a term used for the Azores. Many Azoreans settled in Little Compton in the last decades of the eighteenth century. Azorean immigrants and their descendants frequently chose to be buried out of town in Catholic cemeteries until Our Lady of Fatima Cemetery opened in 1955.

The Oldest Dated Stones
Row 17 Stone 12   Mary Price

Only Mary Price's footstone is legible, but it bears the oldest death date in the Old Burying Ground, 1698. In 1886 local historian Sarah Soule Wilbour circled it with white stones to mark its significance. Those stones are still visible. Mary was related by marriage to Little Compton's first gravestone carver John Stevens who arrived in Little Compton in 1700. Her stone was carved sometime after 1700 and backdated.

Row 17 Stone 13   John Price

John Price's gravestone is dated 1703 and may be the first carved gravestone to be installed in the Old Burying Ground on the Commons. Like his grandmother Mary Price, he was related by marriage to John Stevens who carved this gravestone for the 18-day-old infant. Notice the uneven nature of the lettering, which indicates this is a very early, if not the first, attempt by the stone carver. Stevens was known for his excellent lettering in later years.

Row 16 Stone 22   Mary Graves

John Prices' maternal grandmother is also buried here. Her stone is dated 1700.

Row 27 Stone 20   Efraim Gray

Efraim Gray, the young son of Thomas and Anna Gray, also died in 1698 and shares the distinction of having this cemetery's oldest dated gravestones with Mary Price.

Row 22 Stone 15   Captain Ebenezer Church

Ebenezer Church lived to 100 years. His gravestone displays an excellent example of a nineteenth-century urn and willow design.

Row 22 Stone 22   Captain Oliver P. Earl

Oliver Earl's memorial stone tells the story of his death: *Died at Brent's Island of a fever on the coast of Africa.* Earl was a slave trader working in the last few years of the legal slave trade in the United States. A late-nineteenth century newspaper story directing tourists to the Old Burying Ground's most interesting gravestones offered this bit of gossip:

It is held by some that this inscription does not record the facts in the case, but, as the story goes, Earle enticed on board his vessel two sons of a negro chieftain and they were brought to this country and sold into slavery. When he again visited the place, he was fallen upon and murdered by the chief and his followers.

Row 23 Stone 9   John Dye

John Dye's gravestone is adorned with a grinning imp. It documents a transitional image created by gravestone carver John Stevens I as he switched from skull to angel designs.

Row 23 Stone 8   Sarah Dye

Sarah Dye, John Dye's mother, was buried four years after her son. Her gravestone shows how much progress the carver, John Stevens I, made during those four years.

Row 25 Stone 25   Jonathan Gray

Seventeen-year-old Jonathan Gray was "unfortunately shot in Providence" while he and his friends were stealing peaches from John Fields' orchard in 1825. The teenagers had been raiding the orchard for several nights when Fields' son Albert decided to wait up for the thieves. Albert fatally shot Jonathan in the left eye and was later found guilty of involuntary manslaughter.

The Clap Family

The Clap family is one of Little Compton's very few (perhaps only) eighteenth-century families who did not purchase gravestones from the Stevens Shop in Newport nor use simple fieldstones to mark their family graves. Instead the Claps memorialized their dead with inscriptions roughly carved into fieldstones or gravestones featuring primitive-looking carvings. These unusual stones are attributed to Peter Barker an itinerant stone carver.

Row 25 Stone 6	Mary Clap daughter of Elisha & Leah
Row 25 Stone 7	Leah Clap wife of Elisha
Row 33 Stone 4	Mr. Elisha Clap son of Elisha & Leah
Row 34 Stone 1	Elisha Clap son of Elisha & Elisabeth
Row 34	Missing

*Elizabeth the wife of Elisha Clap.
She died Nov. 18, AD 1758, age 34.*
In 1959 this stone was next to her son Elisha's inscribed fieldstone.

Row 28 Stone 9   Elizabeth Palmer

Elizabeth Palmer's gravestone is the most famous in the Old Burying Ground on the Commons. Years ago, townspeople covered its sides and back with metal to prevent souvenir hunters from chipping pieces from it. It is Elizabeth's unusual epitaph that has drawn all the attention. It reads, "Elizabeth who should have been the wife of Simeon Palmer," and has given rise to all sorts of romantic stories attempting to explain it. In fact, Elizabeth was married to Simeon Palmer; she was his second wife. His first wife Lydia is buried next to Elizabeth with a more typical gravestone. Elizabeth and Simeon had a daughter whom they named after Lydia.

Local legends explain that Simeon "got sun stroke" and began to behave very strangely, insisting that his family eat cat meat. Elizabeth took their daughter, left Simeon and lived with her parents. The stories go on to say that Simeon visited Elizabeth every Sunday and brought her his laundry, which she washed. When Elizabeth died, Simeon had this gravestone carved, intending to insult the woman who refused to live with him with the phrase "should have been." Some stories say that Simeon is buried in an unmarked grave between his two wives, but this is not true. After Elizabeth's death, Simeon married for a third time, sold his pew in the Congregational Church and moved his family to upstate New York. He is buried there.

Row 28 Stone 27   Lovis Devanport (Lois Davenport)

This stone has an excellent grim reaper design by John Bull, a Newport stone carver who apprenticed in the John Stevens Shop.

Row 31 Stone 8   Sarah Simons and Her Brothers

Three-month-old Sarah Simons' stone is unusual because it bears no death date, and it alerts us to the presence of her two unnamed brothers buried on either side of her without inscribed gravestones of their own. Sarah was the youngest of William and Abigail Simons twelve children.

Row 31 Stone 13 William Pabodie

William Pabodie was one of Little Compton's First Proprietors and an early Town Clerk. He was the husband of Elizabeth Alden Pabodie. His gravestone is an excellent example of a John Stevens I skull design and fine block lettering.

Row 31 Stone 14 Elizabeth Alden Pabodie

Elizabeth Alden Pabodie, often called "Betty Alden," was the daughter of Pilgrims John Alden and Priscilla Mullins and is believed to be the first white girl born in New England. She, her husband William Pabodie and a number of their adult children moved to Little Compton in the 1680s and built homes on the Great West Road just south of Taylor's Lane. Upon her death in 1717 Elizabeth was honored with an obituary in the newspaper, a rare occurrence for a woman of her time. The article commented on her many progeny and stated that her "granddaughter Bradford was a grandmother."

Sarah Soule Wilbour, an early local historian, began a fundraising effort to create a monument honoring Betty Alden in 1847 following a centennial celebration of the transfer of Tiverton and Little Compton from Massachusetts to Rhode Island. Betty's original gravestone had sunken into the ground and was difficult to find. Sarah was not successful and put the effort aside. After America's Centennial in 1876, interest in American history grew, and Betty Alden became a celebrated local historical figure. Sarah Soule Wilbour renewed her fundraising efforts, and in 1882 she finally had the necessary funds to install a 12-foot-tall granite obelisk marking Elizabeth's grave and protecting her original gravestone. Newspaper stories from the 1880s reported that many strangers were visiting and that the monument had become a "place of pilgrimage."

Sarah Soule Wilbour's son, Charles Edwin Wilbour, America's first Egyptologist, admires the Betty Alden Monument his mother had installed at Elizabeth Alden Pabodie's gravesite. LCHS Collection.

Row 34 Stones 6–10
The Wood Children

The Wood family lost six children in nine days during an epidemic in 1711/12 and two other children in different years. Each of their gravestones is carved with a John Stevens hanging-toothed skull design. The double gravestones are unusual. The double date results from a change from the Julian calendar to the Gregorian.

Row 36 Stones 13-17
The Five Thomas Churches

Thomas Church (1673-1746), the son of Colonel Benjamin Church and the author of *Entertaining Passages Pertaining to Philip's War*, lost four sons named Thomas and two sons named Benjamin between 1718 and 1749. Their row of box-like ledger stones is unique in the Old Commons Burying Ground. The stones vary in size and style in relation to the age of the person buried. An adult-size ledger stone from the John Stevens shop cost £50 while a typical set of gravestones cost closer to £2. Though they look like tombs, the bodies are buried as usual about six feet below the ground. Thomas Church's second and third wives, Edith Woodman and Sarah Horswell, are also buried here with carved ledger stones. His first wife Sarah Hayman and two small daughters are buried in Bristol. Edith's infant son Thomas, born in May and died August 21, 1718, does not have a grave-stone and is likely buried with his mother who died shortly after his birth.

Row 36 Stone 18
Colonel Benjamin Church

Benjamin Church played a leading role in King Phillip's War and was a First Proprietor of Little Compton. The United States Army Rangers posthumously designated him the first Army Ranger and installed the small "Ranger" plaque on his ledger stone.

Individual minister's gravestones. Photos by Letty Champion.

Rows 36 & 37   The Ministers and their Families

Several of the ministers who served the United Congregational Society and their families are buried in a place of honor close to the church.

Row 36 Stone 30 Reverend Richard Billings

Row 36 Stone 33 Reverend Johnathan Ellis

Row 37 Stone 36 Reverend Mase Shepard

Row 37 Stone 35 John Haskins Shepard

John, the nineteen-year-old son of the Reverend Mase Shepard, has a particularly interesting epitaph: *Here lie the Hopes of a fond Mother & the blasted Expectation of an indulgent Father.* Inscriptions like this indicate that families were especially affected by the death of young adults. At the turn of the nineteenth century Little Compton families, like many other New Englanders, shifted from slate to white marble gravestones.

Row 37 Stone 33 Richard Grinnell

An 1882 newspaper story shared this story about real-life privateer, slave-trader and Revolutionary War veteran Pirate Dick Grinnell:

It is said that on one occasion, as the daughter of the Grand Mogul of India was travelling with her retinue and much treasure in her own vessel, she was captured and murdered by Grinnell and her body thrown overboard. A beautiful white saddle horse belonging to her was also thrown overboard, and as tradition has it, followed the pirate vessel, neighing piteously. The rich and costly saddle and trappings belonging to the horse were brought to Little Compton, where Grinnell had a good estate and where he ended his days. The old man's conscience tortured him, and his conduct was so strange that his house grew to have the reputation of being haunted. On his death bed he declared that he heard the neighing of the Princess' horse, and the watchers by his bedside were quite sure that they heard the sound of its feet. At any rate for aught we know, now he sleeps well.

13
Wilbor Commons Cemetery

South of Commons Road
Gravestones dated from 1775-Present.
Owned by the Wilbor Heirs.
Visitation during daylight hours.
Roadside parking.

This cemetery sits on the homestead farm of Joseph and Ann (Brownell) Wilbor who came to Little Compton around 1684 from Portsmouth, Rhode Island. Joseph was one of four Wilbor brothers who settled in town at that time. Local historian Benjamin Franklin Wilbour writes that Joseph and Ann are buried here. They have no surviving personal gravestones, but a large family monument honors them. The first inscribed gravestones belong to Joseph and Ann's son William Wilbour, who died in 1775, and to his wife Jane who followed in 1780.

In 1838 Joseph and Ann's great-grandson Joseph was the first to ensure that his branch of Little Compton's extensive Wilbor family (multiple spellings) would forever have access to this burying ground. When he gave his homestead farm to his son Walter, Joseph wrote, "reserving however the burying ground a privilege for all the relatives to bury their dead in, and the said Walter and successors to keep the burying place in decent order and repair forever." Though many people exempted their burying grounds from the sale of their property and reserved them for the use of their family, Joseph Wilbor is the only one to designate a caretaker.

Walter took his role as the steward of the family cemetery very seriously. When he died in 1865 he left everything to his wife Lydia for her use during the remainder of her life:

> Except the burial ground which is to remain for the use of all my connections when occasion may require it for to bury the dead during all time to come and it upon the following conditions, namely that each and every grave is to be furnished with good and suitable grave stones by the friends of the deceased as soon as may be after the interment, giving suitable [time] to procure the same. And I do hereby further order and my will and meaning is that my wife procure or cause to be procured

good and substantial grave stones and erect them at my grave with suitable inscriptions upon the same within six months after my decease. And I do also hereby give to my wife and daughters Adeline and Mary the charge of the graveyard desiring and enjoining it upon them to keep the same in good order and not to allow any kind of stock to run in it except horses, and to keep the yard clear of briers weeds etc.

The rules that Walter established, including his ban on plain fieldstone markers, set the tone for the next 150 years and helped ensure that this cemetery was well preserved. Unlike most of Little Compton's family burying grounds, which appear to have been abandoned by present-day family members, the descendants of the people buried here still carefully manage and maintain their family cemetery with the help of the Town of Little Compton. A number of them plan on being buried here themselves someday.

Photo by Bart Brownell.

14
Our Lady of Fatima Cemetery

South of Commons Road
Owned by St. Catherine of Siena Church.
Visitation during daylight hours.
Parking on the paths within the cemetery.
This is an active cemetery. For information call 401-635-4420.

The people of St. Catherine of Siena Church established this cemetery in 1946 when they purchased five acres of land on South of Commons Road from the Rocha family. It is in active use today by members of the parish. Though not as old as Little Compton's other cemeteries, Our Lady of Fatima Cemetery represents an important part of our local history. Catholics arrived in Little Compton in large numbers in the last decades of the nineteenth century, primarily as Azorean farm laborers and domestic workers, and in smaller numbers as Irish servants for summer residents.

Photo by Bart Brownell.

For many years, local Catholics who wished to be buried in consecrated ground had to leave Little Compton for burial in Catholic cemeteries in Fall River and other nearby communities. Our Lady of Fatima Cemetery is named after the apparition of the Virgin Mary in Fatima, Portugal in 1917. It provides all Catholics with a burial place within the community.

The cemetery's gravestones feature a wide variety of designs, from Celtic crosses to Cadillac emblems, reflecting their owners' religious heritage and individual personalities.

Photo by Bart Brownell.

15

BRIGGS-BROWNELL BURYING GROUND

10 North Tupelo Drive – Off South of Commons Road
Gravestones dated 1803-1907.
Owned by the heirs of Mark Anthony Brownell per a 1914 deed.
This cemetery appears to be abandoned by the family.
Visitation during daylight hours.
Park on North Tupelo Drive. Enter yard on foot. Gate is in the northeast corner.

Historic cemeteries can tell many different stories. This one tells the poignant story of a concerned father and a resilient mother.

Captain Cornelius Briggs, a Revolutionary War veteran, wrote his will in 1802 when he was 60 years old, a reasonable age for men of his time to put their affairs in order. However, because of a second marriage Cornelius was the father of young children ages eight, seven and four. He took extra care in his will to ensure that they and his wife Fallee Brownell, who was fourteen years his junior, would be secure and comfortable after his death. To complicate matters, Cornelius had only one son, seven-year-old Cornelius Junior. At that time, fathers, with few exceptions, left their real estate to their sons and their moveable property to their daughters. Cornelius Senior's will ultimately gave all of his real estate to his son Cornelius when he reached adulthood, but it also had to ensure that Fallee and their young daughters were provided for until they died or married. Understanding the very real threat of death in the early-nineteenth century, Cornelius wrote a variety of contingencies into his will in case any of his children died before they reached adulthood and could take possession of their inheritances. It was a good thing he did.

When Cornelius died in 1803, Fallee could have buried him with his first wife Mary Brownell in the Briggs family burying ground. Instead, she chose to bury him on their own homestead farm and so established this burying ground that would be used by three generations of their family.

Photo by Bart Brownell.

Fallee served as her husband's executrix and as guardian for her children. Not every woman was capable of doing this because it was necessary to know how to write and to do math in order to submit regular reports to the Town Council. Fallee could do both. In fact, in addition to administering her husband's estate, she also finished settling her father-in law William Brigg's affairs during her first few months of widowhood.

Fallee was an excellent manager, petitioning the Town Council and ultimately the state's General Assembly on more than one occasion to sell just enough of her husband's real estate to pay his debts and the family expenses, while still preserving a homestead farm of sufficient size to support herself and her three children.

Sadly, in 1819 Fallee had to play the role of executrix once again when her only son Cornelius died at the age of 24 without an heir. Now her husband's contingencies came into play, and she and her daughters became the farm's owners. Together Cornelius Senior's meticulous planning and Fallee's careful management ensured their farm provided dowries for their daughters and a comfortable living for Fallee until her death in 1832.

In her will Fallee gave her 60-acre portion of the farm containing the family burial ground to her grandson Cornelius Briggs Brownell. Eighty-two years later in 1914 her great grandson Mark Anthony Brownell sold it out of the family, "hereby reserving the family burial lot on said premise and a right to pass and repass to and from the same to the descendants or relatives of those buried therein." Instead of joining his ancestors, Mark Anthony chose to be buried in the Old Burying Ground on the Commons.

16

BRIGGS BURYING GROUND

Shaw Road
Gravestones dated 1711-1857.
Owned and maintained by the family.
No visitation.

The Briggs homestead farm is one of Little Compton's few properties still owned by the descendants of the English colonists who established it around

Photo by Bart Brownell.

1680. The family burying ground ceased being used after 1857, but its handsomely carved gravestones survive today in a new, more protected location.

William Briggs (1718-1802) and his wife Abishag Records (1716-1790) were the third generation of Briggs to live on the farm. William wrote about the family burying ground in his will in a way that helps us understand how it developed and changed over time.

> ITEM - *& my will further more is & I do hereby reserve one quarter on an acre of ground in my farm where I now dwell and give it for a Burying place for my relations to bury their dead in if they see cause, which quarter of acre is where the graves now are. Also I give my relations that bury their dead there full power and authority to fence off sd burying place or Quarter of Acre, which Quarter of Arce shall extend from the highway southward until it comprehends and takes in the Quarter of acre which I gave to be appropriated forever for that use.*

William's will tells us, and gravestone dates confirm, that the Briggs Burying Ground already contained graves by 1802, and that it was unfenced at that time. Many family burying grounds started in this way and were eventually walled in by later generations. With a quarter-acre, William set aside a significantly large piece of land for a burying ground. He expected many generations of his large, extended family to make use of it, and they did for about 150 years.

The cemetery's location is also of interest. There were no set rules regarding the location of family burying grounds. Some families, like the Briggs, placed them adjacent to established roads. This enabled family members to access the burying ground without disturbing the farmer's field. It also provided passersby the opportunity to see the burying ground and remember the dead or perhaps comment on the quality of the gravestones. Other families, like the Wilbors on West Main Road (LC009) and Long Highway (LC027), set their burying grounds farther back on their properties in more private locations that were more difficult to reach.

At some point in the first half of the twentieth century the Briggs descendants made the decision to move their ancestors' gravestones back from the road to a more private, walled, location further south on the property. All of the inscribed gravestones bear the Briggs surname with the exception of Deborah Carr's. Deborah was born a Briggs, outlived two husbands and returned to her family home in her old age.

The Briggs Burying Ground reflects many of the changes in Little Compton gravestones over time. It begins with slate stones with angels from the John Stevens Shop in Newport dated from the 1710s through the Revolution, then switches to the Throop Shop in Bristol because of the British occupation in Newport, then moves to the urn designs made by a wide variety of stone carvers around the turn of the nineteenth century, and finally, ends with the inscribed but unornamented marble stones popular in the mid-nineteenth century. The current arrangement of the stones reflects decisions made by the people who moved them and may or may not represent their placement in their original location.

Photo by Bart Brownell.

17

Joseph & Deborah Brownell Burying Ground

52D Grange Avenue
Gravestones dated 1803-1881 and fieldstones.
This lot appears to be abandoned by the family.
Visitation during daylight hours.
Park on the grass near the burying ground.

Cemeteries require regular repair and maintenance. Without them, stones topple and sometimes break, and vegetation grows impenetrable. At the end of the twentieth century, a number of Little Compton's historic cemeteries had been abandoned and were in terrible condition. This Brownell family burying ground was so overgrown, its gravestones were barely visible.

In the 1990s Little Compton Historical Society volunteers Helen and Fred Bridge surveyed and repaired many of Little Compton's historic cemeteries, including this one. In addition to physical repairs, they recorded the data on the gravestones and joined forces with the Rhode Island Historical Cemetery Commission to help create a database that is still in use today. Fred took the lead on repair, while Helen managed the data and shared it with John Sterling of the Rhode Island Historical Cemetery Commission. These repaired cemeteries remain in good, accessible condition today because of the attentive maintenance of the Town of Little Compton. Around 2010, Cemetery Commission volunteer Letty Champion photographed almost all of Little Compton's historic gravestones and added their images to the database making it the powerful research tool it is today. (Visit rihistoriccemeteries.org)

These turn-of-the-twenty-first-century efforts were not the first time local volunteers took an interest in preserving Little Compton's cemeteries and the valuable historical information they contain. Benjamin Franklin Wilbour spent years transcribing Little Compton's gravestones in the early decades of the twentieth century and then retraced his steps in 1959 with the help of genealogist Waldo Chamberlain Sprague to confirm and improve his work. The

Before repairs in the 1990s. Photo by Fred Bridge.

New England Historical and Genealogical Society published their transcriptions in 1961. Because gravestones break or are removed, because carvings fade, and because Little Compton's vital records are incomplete, these gravestone transcriptions are sometimes the only evidence we have of a person.

Based on the gravestones that survive in this lot, it appears that Joseph Brownell (1744-1824) and his wife Deborah Briggs (1748-1840) established this cemetery in 1803 to bury their son Joseph B. Brownell (b. 1780) who died when he was 23 years old. However, surviving inscribed gravestones often do not tell a complete family story. Birth records show that Joseph and Deborah had a young daughter named Elizabeth in 1776. This child died sometime before the birth of her sister, also named Elizabeth in 1779. The first Elizabeth does not have a surviving inscribed gravestone. We cannot know for sure if she was buried, here or elsewhere, with a simple fieldstone or if sometime since her death an inscribed stone was destroyed or lost. Benjamin Franklin Wilbour has no record of her in his early-twentieth century transcriptions.

We do know a little bit more about her brother Isaac's gravestone. It was intact when B.F. Wilbour did his transcriptions, reading: *Isaac Brownell died May 16, 1818 in his 46th year.* We also see in the Rhode Island Historical Cemetery Commission photograph below that Isaac's gravestone was broken in 2010 and would have been difficult if not impossible to identify as Isaac's without B.F. Wilbour's transcriptions. The design of Isaac's gravestone is a match for his brother Joseph B.'s stone, a strong indication that the family ordered and installed both stones at the same time, long after Joseph's death.

Photo by Letty Champion.

Without the transcriptions and the database photographs, it would be easy to assume that Isaac never had a gravestone and tempting to speculate why his family did not provide him with one. This, of course, would be incorrect and is important to keep in mind when visiting other cemeteries. We cannot say for certain that someone did not have an inscribed gravestone, only that there is no surviving stone today.

B.F. Wilbour recorded another stone here that is missing today, a marker inscribed: Elizabeth daughter of Captain Owen Wilber and Mary his wife died Sept 7, 1822 aged 16 mos. This Elizabeth was Joseph and Deborah's granddaughter. Her mother Mary died four years later and has no surviving gravestone. It is possible that she is buried here along with two other daughters, Hannah and Mary, who also died in infancy. Mary's husband Captain Owen Wilber remarried and is buried in the Old Burying Ground on the Commons.

The last known burial here was for Amie Ann Wilbor Brownell (1836-1881) the wife of Joseph and Deborah's grandson Albert Brownell (1834-1912). After Amie's death, Albert mortgaged the farm to Annie W. Brownell (likely a relative, but the relationship is unknown) and defaulted on the loan in 1893. When he signed the property over to Annie, he excepted the family burying ground from the deed and reserved the right to pass and repass to it. Albert remarried and moved to Westport, choosing to be buried in the Beech Grove Cemetery there.

Photo by Bart Brownell.

18

Shaw-Seabury Cemetery

27 Butts Rock Road, Chase Point
Gravestones dated 1825-1991 and numerous undated stones.
Owned by the heirs of John and Maria (Shaw) Seabury per a 1954 deed.
Roadside parking.

In addition to the stone walls that surround so many of Little Compton's burying grounds, the Shaw-Seabury Cemetery is surrounded by a tall hedge that makes it feel like a secret place. Once inside, visitors see a family cemetery unlike any other in the community. All of its gravestones face north-south instead of east-west, and 30 of them are small, dark-brown rectangles with no inscriptions.

The Shaws farmed this land since their arrival in Little Compton in the late 1600s. It is possible that this cemetery served them and their enslaved people since that time. The early generations of Shaws, like so many Little Compton residents, probably buried their dead with uninscribed fieldstones. Those burials would have been oriented east to west like every other eighteenth- and early-nineteenth-century grave in Little Compton. At some point those fieldstones were removed and replaced by the 30 rectangular stones we see today, all installed in a north-south direction. This change probably took place sometime after the Shaw farm was sold out of the family in 1954 and developed into what we now know as the Chace Point neighborhood. In his 1959 report, local historian Benjamin Franklin Wilbour records "about 30 unmarked stones here." He did not do this for fieldstones, so it is very likely that the new stones were in place by 1959.

The earliest inscribed gravestones in the cemetery belong to the family of the Honorable Jediah Shaw (1777-1852) and his wife Rhoda Manchester Slocum (1786-1842). Jediah was a member of the fifth generation of Shaws to live in Little Compton. Rhoda was a widow when she married Jediah in 1813. All of the people buried here with gravestones dated between 1825 and 1933 are Jediah and Rhoda's children, grandchildren, great-grandchildren and their spouses.

John Seabury joined the family in 1836 when he married Jediah and Rhoda's daughter Maria. Ownership of the 104-acre farm and its cemetery passed to the Seaburys, and in 1954 their heirs sold it to the Chace family excepting "the Seabury Burial Lot" from the sale. In 1991 and 1989 Peter Van Cleve Shaw and his wife Eileen Smith Shaw chose to be buried here, the first burials in over 50 years.

Photo by Bart Brownell.

19

HENRY HEAD SR. BURYING GROUND

Near 41 Maple Ave
Gravestones dated 1716-1872 and fieldstones.
Owned by the Head heirs per William Head's 1783 will.
This lot appears to be abandoned by the family.
Roadside parking.

Here lie rebels and rascals.

Henry Head and his associates paid two calls on Little Compton's tax collector Daniel Eaton. At the first, in early November 1692, Henry and company ambushed Constable Eaton, freeing a friend he had detained for nonpayment. Two weeks later, their second visit, with "swords, staves, gunns and clubbs" in hand, convinced Eaton to forgo collecting Massachusetts state taxes from Little Compton men in the near future. Henry and his co-conspirators wanted out of cash-strapped Massachusetts and into Rhode Island, and they were willing to die to accomplish it. After a days-long stand-off between the would-be Rhode Islanders and the Massachusetts law enforcement sent to arrest them, Henry stood down and no lives were lost.

Convicted of "riot, rout, and other high misdemeanors," he was jailed, fined, and released. Henry Head (1647-1716) went to his grave paying Massachusetts taxes. Henry's slate gravestone was carved by the Stevens Shop in Newport. His wife Elizabeth Ketchum (1654-1748) is probably buried here with uninscribed stones.

The antics of several of Henry and Elizabeth's young adult offspring are preserved in court records. While in their early twenties, daughters Mary (b. 1711) and Elizabeth (b. 1716) broke into Jonathan Record's shop, stole some of his tools and threw them down a well. Where they and their husbands are buried is unknown. Henry's sons, Benjamin and Henry Junior, and their enslaved man Jeffry were accused of stealing a honey-filled beehive from the minister's wife.

Photo by Bart Brownell.

Benjamin (1687-1717) is buried here with a slate Stevens Shop stone. His wife, Deborah Briggs Head Carr (1693-1773) is buried at the Briggs Lot (LC016). Benjamin and Deborah's only child, William (1715-1784) reserved this burying ground in his will. He and his wife, Elizabeth Manchester (born c. 1715) seem to have kept a low profile; if they are buried here, their gravestones are uninscribed or lost.

Neighbors complained of troublesome "mal conduct" by William and Elizabeth's grandsons Job and Benjamin Head. The Town Council assigned a guardian to manage the brothers' finances to prevent them becoming a burden to the town. Benjamin reformed, and the Town Council restored his privileges. He wasn't called to task for such conduct again. He and his wife, Abigail Crapo (1777-1860), are buried here. His is the slate stone carved by the Cooley Shop of Providence. Hers is of marble. Benjamin's brother Job Head (c. 1767) and their parents, Benjamin (1744-1833) and Eliphal Palmer (c. 1740) have no known gravestones.

Palmer Head (1797-1872) was married to Ruth Manley (1800-1868) for fifty years. But tongues probably wagged when the widower of eight months married Bridgett O'Connell Powers (1824-1909) a widowed "house servant" 27 years his junior. Palmer's will instructed his children to erect gravestones for himself and Ruth. He is buried here with his parents Benjamin and Abigail. Ruth is buried in the Manley lot. When Bridgett Head died in 1909 she was buried here. The Town Council covered the cost of her burial but not the cost of inscribed gravestones. Bridgett is the last known burial in this lot.

Photo by Bart Brownell.

20

George & Elizabeth Brownell Burying Ground

21 Maple Avenue
Gravestones dated 1814-1879.
Owned by the heirs of George Brownell per his 1824 will.
This lot appears to have abandoned by the family.
Visitation during daylight hours.
Enter the laneway at 21 C & D Maple Avenue.
Park on the grass near the burying ground.

Little Compton's family burying grounds were quiet corners surrounded by busy working farms. In 1843 Ezra Brownell used land evidence records to make sure his brothers and their wives felt welcome using the burying ground on the farm he inherited from his parents, but he also took the time to make sure they did so carefully.

Ezra was concerned that visits to the graves or new burials, especially if a cart was used to carry the coffin, would damage the crops in his field or disrupt his business in other ways. He wrote:

> I give to all the children and grandchildren of my father the right to pass
> from the gate by the road through the door yard and meadow south of
> the house to the burial ground gate for the purpose of burying their dead
> except when the said meadow shall have a crop of corn or other grain
> standing thereon, then the said Ezra Brownell and my heirs and assigns
> do agree to furnish a proper and convenient pass to said burial ground on
> some other part of my farm, they doing as little damage as may be.

Ezra's house faced what is now called John Simmons Road, and his farm-
land stretched to the south bounded on the east by Maple Avenue. Ezra's
father George established the family burying ground in 1824 when he
chose to bury his wife Elizabeth Peckham Brownell to the south of the
house in the southeast corner of one of his fields. The field had walls of
rough granite stones to the south and east of Elizabeth's grave, but to the
north and west the burial ground was open to the field at that time. After
Elizabeth's death George wrote a codicil to his will giving his children the
right to be buried next to their mother, reserving the area as a burying
ground forever, and determining that it should measure 3 rods square (49.5
feet square).

George's descendants eventually walled in the cemetery. They left the
rough yellow granite field walls to the east and south but built the burying
ground's north and west walls more carefully using flat gray slate and
schist stones that fit together tightly creating a much finer wall. Time has
taken its toll on all four sides of the cemetery walls, but the difference
between the older field walls and the walls built specifically for the cemetery
can still be seen today.

One of the most interesting stones in the burying ground is one of the
smallest. It reads:

> An Infant Son
> of Ezra & Lucy
> Brownell
> Died June 7, 1814
> aged 18 days;
> & was buried
> in the Wilbor
> Burying Place

This is a memorial stone not a gravestone. The baby is buried in the Old
Wilbor Burying Ground at the Wilbor House Museum with an uninscribed

fieldstone. His mother Lucy grew up there. She may have even given birth to him there with the help of her mother and other female relatives. It is curious that even though this child survived for eighteen days his parents did not use a name on his memorial stone. He may have been very frail from the moment of birth, and so not named. Ezra and Lucy had this stone made so that their only son would be honored in the same way they honored their two daughters buried here: Lucy W., died 1832, age two months and Priscilla W., died 1838, age 19.

21

STEPHEN & PRISCILLA SIMMONS LOT

Near 9 Peckham Road.
Gravestones dated 1815-1891.
This lot appears to be abandoned by the family.
Limited roadside parking across the street.
Be cautious of the hill and corner.

Stephen and Priscilla (Head) Simmons are the central figures in this small family burying ground. Both lived unusually long lives, Stephen dying at 88 in 1861, and Priscilla at 98 in 1875. Each of the people buried here connect to them in some way. Their nine-year-old daughter Julia Ann has the earliest inscribed stone dated 1815. Stephen and Priscilla's youngest child, born two years after Julia Ann's death and a surprising thirteen years after the birth of their previous child, was also named Julia Ann. She, too, is buried here, under her married name Julia A. Dyer. Hers is the newest stone in the burying ground, dated 1891. Julia Dyer's first husband, Job Slocum died in 1851 and is buried here with his in-laws, which is very likely why Julia selected this as her final resting place. However, she chose to bury her second husband Deacon John Dyer, Jr., who died in 1880, in the Pleasant View Cemetery near the Old Stone Church in Tiverton, perhaps near his first wife.

Pardon Simmons, a goldsmith and Stephen's older brother, died in 1841, and like Julia Ann Dyer also raises interesting questions about why husbands and wives chose to be buried together or separately. In his will Pardon

Photo by Bart Brownell.

designated his friend Christopher Brown as executor and directed him to:

erect or cause to be erected a decent pair of gravestones to my grave and also a similar pair to the grave of my first wife Hannah Simmons in one year after my decease.

Brown honored his friend's wishes and purchased two matching sets of handsome slate headstones and footstones with a graceful willow and obelisk design, one set for Pardon's grave on Peckham Road and one for Hannah's in the Old Burying Ground on the Commons. Pardon's second wife Betsey is also buried in the Old Burying Ground but with a plain marble stone that is unusual because it lists only her age of 84 and not the year of her death. Pardon does not mention Betsey in his will, which is normally a sign that a wife is already dead. However, if this was true Betsey would have been at least ten years older than Pardon, and that is unlikely. Betsey's gravestone is also a more modern design than Pardon's, another clue that she outlived him. It seems that he purposely chose not to remember her in his will, and that they chose not to be buried together.

Photo by Bart Brownell.

22

PEARCE LOTS

24 Austin Lane, off Burchard Avenue
Gravestones dated 1775-1866 and numerous fieldstones.
Owned by the Pearce heirs.
This lot appears to be abandoned by the family.
Visitation during daylight hours.
Enter on foot via driveway of 24 Austin Lane.
Park on cul-de-sac leaving room to pass. Do not block driveways.
Do not park on grass.

The Pearces (also "Pierce," both pronounced "Purse" in Little Compton) were a large Little Compton family with broad landholdings concentrated in the Burchard Avenue, Long Highway and East Main Road areas. The extended family shared a burial ground that was once reached by a long laneway leading west from the Stone School House on Long Highway. Burchard Avenue did not exist at that time but now provides the only access to the lots. Community volunteers restored the Pearce Lots in the 1990s.

This large burying ground is actually two separate lots, one large rectangle to the east and a smaller rectangle to the west, with a small square area and a pathway in between. The purpose of the small square area is unclear, but the inscribed gravestones show us that the lot to the west is newer than the rest of the burying ground and is specific to the family of Benjamin (1784-1869) and Sarah (1788-1866) Pearce. The first Pearces arrived in Little Compton from Portsmouth, Rhode Island in the 1680s. The eastern lot contains numerous uninscribed stones and was probably established early in the eighteenth century. Its oldest dated stone reads 1775.

As the family burying ground filled, Benjamin and Sarah decided to create their own nearby, prompted, as often happened, by the death of a grandchild. The family buried one-year old Ann Pearce, the daughter of Rouse and Comfort Maria Pearce, in 1853. Her big brother Franklin joined her in 1857 when he was six.

It was the custom in many Little Compton family burying grounds for the patriarch and matriarch of the family to be buried in a place of prominence, often in the center and to the west of the lot with their younger family members fanning out behind them to the east. Even though grandchildren were the first to be buried here, the family planned ahead, reserving this special location at the west end of the new lot for Benjamin and Sarah's future use.

The children's mother Comfort Maria (1832-1862) appears to be the first adult buried with them, followed by their aunt Lucy Blake Pearce (1822-1866) and their grandmother Sarah in 1866. Each of these women died before their husband and was memorialized by a handsome marble stone with a touching epitaph. Comfort's husband Rouse and Lucy's husband James remarried and have no known gravestones in the area.

Patriarch Benjamin died three years after his wife Sarah and was buried in his reserved place of honor next to her, but his grave is marked only by an uninscribed stone. Only in rare cases, like this one, do we have enough clues to identify someone buried with an uninscribed stone.

There are dozens of uninscribed stones in the larger, older part of the Pearce burying ground marking the resting places of generations of Pearces, their in-laws and perhaps their enslaved people. The use of fieldstone markers or unmarked graves continued in Little Compton into the twentieth century. Town records show that Deborah Pierce was buried here in 1911. She has no surviving inscribed gravestone and may have been buried without one. There are, however, a number of carved stones that do survive here, some of them very beautiful. The stone for 26-year-old Benjamin Pearce who died in 1822 invites us to:

Stop traveler and drop a tear
If per chance you linger here
For one cut down in life's gay bloom
and laid within the silent tomb,
my prospects late were fair as thine
and soon thy fate may be like mine.

Only one inscribed stone is for a person with a surname other than Pearce. Nathaniel Tompkins (1748-1775) married Phebe Pearce in 1774. He died a year later, two months before their son Nathaniel was born. Forty-one years later, Nathaniel replaced his father's original grave marker, probably a fieldstone, with a marble stone memorializing the father he never met and stating, "erected by his son Nathaniel 1816." Local family members remembered the exact locations of their loved ones' graves for decades even without the benefit of inscribed stones, but over the generations most of these memories have been lost.

Photo by Bart Brownell.

23

HUNT BURYING GROUND

Colebrook Road near Long Highway
One gravestone dated 1820 and numerous fieldstones.
Owned by the heirs of Nathaniel Hunt per his 1832 deed to his son Dennis.
This burying ground appears to be abandoned by the family.
Visitation during daylight hours.
Parking in the adjacent Simmons Mill parking area.

The Hunt family burying ground contains approximately 18 graves. Each one is marked by a mound of earth covered with lush green moss. Many have a headstone and footstone of uncarved granite fieldstones. Except for a single carved stone, it is impossible to know for sure who is buried here, but based on deeds for the the stone farmhouse to the east, we believe that the families of three generations of Hunts are at rest here: Adam (1745-c. 1820) and Ruth (Jamison) (b. 1747) Hunt; their son and daughter-in-law Nathan (1786-1847) and Almy (Coggeshall) (b.1789) Hunt; and their grandson Dennis (1810-1894) and his wives Mary Ann Coggeshall and Angeline Manchester (b.1813).

Because adult unmarried daughters so frequently lived with their parents, it is very likely that Adam and Ruth's three daughters Rhoda (b. 1770), Elizabeth (b. 1775) and Abigail (b. 1782) are buried here along with their parents.

The lot's one inscribed gravestone belongs to Adam and Ruth's granddaughter Elizabeth Wilbor (1795-1820), the daughter of Zilpha Hunt and her husband Thomas Church Wilbour who lived on Long Highway to the south. Young adult granddaughters often lived with their grandparents as companions and helpers, and Elizabeth may have been living here when she

Photo by Bart Brownell.

died. Why 24-year-old Elizabeth was buried with an inscribed gravestone while all the other family members were not, is unknown. Early American families often seem especially struck by the death of a young adult because of the loss of potential those deaths represented. They would often purchase more elaborate gravestones for young adults than they did for small children. This may be the case with Elizabeth, however, her half-sister Angeline was 16 when she died a year after Elizabeth, and she does not have a surviving gravestone.

It is also possible that Elizabeth's mother Zilpha (1773-1796) is buried here. Some young wives were buried in their parents' burial grounds rather than with their in-laws.

Zilpha appears to have died in connection with the birth of her fourth child. Two more of her children may be buried here, James (b. 1794) and Zilpha II (b. 1796). After Zilpha's death Thomas married her younger sister Ruth Hunt II, and they proceeded to have 15 children, three of whom died young and may be here as well: Angeline (1805-1821), Lydia (b. 1810), and Betsey. They may also be buried in the Wilbor-Tripp Burying Ground on Long Highway, another burying ground with numerous fieldstone markers (see page 75).

The Hunts, like many eighteenth-century Little Compton residents, did not record the deaths of family members with the Town Clerk, so without inscribed gravestones it is very difficult or even impossible to determine their death dates. This is especially true for the female members of the family who are less likely to have probate documents that contain an approximate death date.

Because so much of our local genealogy is taken directly from Little Compton's gravestones, people buried with inscribed stones tend to be remembered while those buried without inscribed stones tend to be forgotten.

24

ADAMSVILLE CEMETERY

Adamsville Hill at the corner of Colebrook and John Dyer Roads
Gravestones dated 1821-1920 and a few fieldstones.
Owned by the heirs of Peleg Manchester per an 1855 deed.
This cemetery appears to be abandoned by the heirs.
Visitation during daylight hours.
Roadside parking at the corner of Colebrook Road and John Dyer Roads.
Do not park on Colebrook Road or the private driveway to the east.
Picnic table and benches provided by Eagle Scout Elisha Wilson,
  Little Compton Boy Scout Troop 29.

This one-acre cemetery served the members of Adamsville's Christian Baptist Meeting House. The church's granite foundation stones can still be seen in the small lot to the north of the cemetery. Local Baptists established this church in the early 1800s as an offshoot of the Old Stone Baptist Church in Tiverton. The cemetery officially came into existence in 1855

The Adamsville Baptist Church by Joseph Shoemaker, c. 1820. Courtesy of Dr. John Bergland.

when Peleg Manchester bought the lot from Allen and Sarah Gifford "to be used for a Burying Ground and no other purpose," but a large number of graves dated prior to the purchase date indicate that the cemetery may have been in use before then. A twenty-six-member church committee sold the church in 1862, and the building eventually became Adamsville School House No. 6. The church members' descendants continued to bury their loved ones here for another 60 years. No sales documents for the cemetery have been found, indicating that it still belongs to the heirs of Peleg Manchester.

The Adamsville Cemetery combines some of the old customs used in the Old Burying Ground on the Commons, established in 1677, with some of the newer customs of the Union Cemetery, established in 1855. The graves in the Adamsville Cemetery are oriented east to west, just as they are in the Old Burying Ground, but the Adamsville Cemetery also contains distinct family burial plots like those used by the Union Cemetery. In Adamsville many of the family plots are clearly marked by granite corner posts that once had chains or fence rails to separate them from the rest of the cemetery.

One plot in the middle of the cemetery contains the remains of the family of Francis Veray (1803-1868) and his wife Lydia Simmons (1804-1885). Some sources say that Francis Veray was a minister for the Christian Baptist Church. Francis was born in the Azores and was one of Little Compton's first Portuguese immigrants, probably the first to own land. He arrived in the community prior to his marriage to Lydia Simmons in 1833, and he and Lydia owned a farm at the east end of Peckham Road near his in-laws. Though author David Patten (1888-1975) claims that his child-hood playmate Mamie d'Azeveda was the first Portuguese girl born in Little Compton, Francis and Lydia's daughter, Lydia Frances Veray Lewis (1836-1896) is a much more likely candidate for that title and is buried here in her parents' plot.

Many different surnames appear on the gravestones here, especially those with strong connections to the village of Adamsville: Taber, Gifford, Dyer, Manchester and Cook to name a few. Though this cemetery appears to have room for many more burials, around the turn of the twentieth century most Adamsville residents chose to be buried in the large Pleasant View Cemetery adjacent to the Old Stone Baptist Church just over the Tiverton-Little Compton line.

The Veray family plot. Photo by Marjory O'Toole.

Photo by Bart Brownell.

25

WILBOR-GIFFORD
BURYING GROUND

25 Amesbury Lane
Gravestones dated 1803-1915 and numerous fieldstones.
Owned by the heirs of Oliver C. Wilbor per their 1916 deed.
This cemetery appears to be abandoned by the family.
Accessed via private property.
Visitation by appointment only. Contact seanmullaney@comcast.net.

At first glance the Wilbor–Gifford Burying Ground contains a confusing mix of people. The descendants of Enos and Mary Gifford are buried to the south while the descendants of Brownell and Esther Wilbor are buried to the north in this single, walled lot. The large number of uninscribed fieldstone markers that run along the western wall of the burying ground provide a clue that the family cemetery is older than its inscribed stones. If we go back one generation, we see that Mary Wilbor Gifford (1740-1803) and Brownell Wilbor (1755-1783) were siblings, and that everyone buried here either descends from their parents Isaac and Mary (Brownell) Wilbor or relates to them by marriage.

Isaac Wilbor (1712-1793) was the youngest child of Samuel and Mary Wilbor the original owners of the house that is now the Wilbor House Museum. In his 1793 will, Isaac left this 80-acre farm to his youngest son Brownell. Isaac and Mary's two older boys already had farms of their own. It was very common for Little Compton parents to help their first two or three sons establish their own farms in the community and to keep a younger son at home to help them in their old age. The youngest son would sometimes end up with a farm that was even better than his brothers, but in return he inherited the responsibility of caring for all the dependent members of the family, most often his widowed mother and unmarried sisters. Isaac gave his wife Mary and his unmarried daughters Susannah and Elizabeth the right to use the west end of his house as long as they remained unmarried and all of his household goods. Brownell and his family had the east end of the house.

Brownell's married sisters were treated very differently in their father's will. They each received 100 silver dollars. From a twentieth-first-century perspective the difference in inheritances for sons and daughters may seem unfair, but in historical terms inheritances are more equal than we imagine. Traditionally, sons received real estate either at the time of their marriage or at the time of their father's death while daughters received moveable property, household items they could take with them to their new homes when they married. In early America land was cheap and household items, especially textiles, were very expensive. Parents worked hard to make sure both their sons and daughters, married or not, lived a comfortable adult life.

Isaac's married daughter Mary lived across the street with her husband Enos Gifford. Enos purchased their 33-acre farm from Mary's first cousin Eseck Wilbor in 1771. Enos was a weaver and had an outbuilding that he referred to as a "loom house" on his property. When Mary died in 1803 at the age of 63, Enos married her 49-year-old sister Susannah seven months later. Susannah (1754-1823) moved from her brother Brownell's house across the street to Enos' house bringing the valuable household goods she inherited from her father with her.

The Giffords and Dyers buried here descend from Mary and Enos. Their unmarried daughter Hannah Gifford (1782-1856) chose to be buried in the Adamsville Cemetery (LC024) but made sure in her will that her older sister Phillis (1765-1823) received a gravestone in this burying ground. The Wilbors, Records and Woodmans descend from Brownell and Esther Wilbor. Notably, three of their daughters married three Woodman brothers.

26

TABER-HOXIE-MANCHESTER CEMETERY

Near 26 Pottersville Road
Gravestones dated 1823-1915.
This cemetery appears to be abandoned by the family.
Roadside parking.

The name alone alerts visitors that a variety of families once buried their loved ones in this elegant little cemetery that followed the nineteenth-century fashion of facing gravestones in a variety of directions. Its unusual stones walls, made of finely fitted stones in the back and long granite blocks in the front, are unique in Little Compton. They help shield the fact that,

Photo by Bart Brownell.

as in many of Little Compton's historic cemeteries, the gravestones here are badly in need of repair. A number of them have fallen, and most of the footstones have been removed and now rest against the wall.

After living in Newport, Kingstown and Nantucket, Peleg Hoxie (1754-1834) settled his family in Little Compton in the 1790s. He had the sad task of establishing this burying ground for two of his grandchildren who died in 1823: the unnamed infant daughter of his son Christopher and the 19-year-old son of his daughter Frances Hoxie Manchester, named Christopher after his uncle.

The next apparent burial, ten years later, was also for a child and stretched the definition of extended family to include Peleg's son-in-law John Dyer's

Photo by Bart Brownell.

great-niece, Susannah Palmer, age one. Susannah's brother and parents also appear to be buried here and are memorialized on a large obelisk for the Palmer family. Her grandparents Benjamin and Abigail (Dyer) Tabor have more traditional nineteenth-century gravestones.

The remaining gravestones mark the graves of Peleg's second wife Mary Waite of Tiverton (1755-1834), his children, grandchildren and great-grandchildren. Mary's gravestone not only identifies her as Peleg's wife but also as the daughter of John and Mary Waite of Tiverton, even though she was 78 years old at the time of her death. Adult women are frequently identified in relation to their husbands or fathers on historic gravestones. It is unusual for both relationships to be listed unless the woman was very young. Male children and young adult men are also often identified in relation to their father or both parents. Adult men, single or married, are usually identified only as themselves.

Inscriptions with relationship clues are very helpful to family members and genealogists trying to untangle the often complicated web of family connections represented in a private burying ground. Three-year-old Charles Richmond Osgood would seem out of place in the Hoxie, Taber, Manchester Cemetery without his inscription connecting him to his parents Edward and Mary Ann Osgood. With this detailed inscription and genealogical records, we can connect Charles back to his great-grandfather Peleg Hoxie through his mother Mary Ann Manchester Osgood and his grandmother Frances Hoxie Manchester, the daughter of Peleg.

Photo by Bart Brownell.

27

WILBOR-TRIPP BURYING GROUNDS

482 Long Highway
Gravestones dated 1762-1880 and numerous fieldstones.
The Wilbor lot is owned by the heirs of Francis Wilbor per his 1809 deed.
The Tripp lot is privately owned.
These cemeteries appear to be abandoned by the families.
Surrounded by private property. Private laneway.
Visitation by appointment only. Contact Calyn Acebes at
*   calynacebes@yahoo.com or 401-239-9888.*

Today visitors to the Wilbor-Tripp cemeteries see two large burying grounds joined at one end by the remnants of a stone wall. Each lot measures four-rods square (approximately 62 feet square). Prior to 1850, there was only one burying ground here, a single four-rod-square lot originally owned by John (b. 1658) and Hannah Wilbor and their descendants. John and Hannah were among Little Compton's first English settlers. They and their son John (1683-1747) and his first and second wives,

Margaret Brownell and Sarah Palmer (b. 1689), are all very likely buried here with uninscribed fieldstones. In the third generation we see a single carved gravestone for Mary the wife of Aaron Willbur (various spellings) who died in 1762 at the age of 38. The decision to bury Mary with a carved grave-stone may have been influenced by her parents Thomas and Sarah Church. While early generations of Wilbors were buried with fieldstone markers, members of Little Compton's influential Church family typically purchased gravestones from the John Stevens Shop in Newport.

Captain Aaron Wilbor (1724-1802) and at least four of his five sons served in the American Revolution. Their pension records show that Captain Aaron and Aaron Junior were at the Battle of Bunker Hill. Aaron Junior and his brother Francis were part of Sullivan's Expedition to rid Newport of the British occupation. Thomas Church Wilbor served over 15 months as both a soldier and a seaman in Rhode Island and Massachusetts. Youngest son John served in Colonel Olney's Rhode Island Regiment for three years and was discharged at Saratoga, New York. Son Benjamin also served according to local historian Benjamin Franklin Wilbor, but no available military records are a good match for this Benjamin Wilbour. None of these men have surviving gravestones in Little Compton.

Census records show that an enslaved woman lived in Aaron's household in 1774 and that he owned an enslaved person in 1790, while his probate records show no enslaved people in 1802. Assuming it is the same woman in both censuses, she is also probably buried here without an inscribed stone.

In addition to Mary Wilbor's inscribed gravestone, the Wilbor lot contains just one more carved stone. It has weathered so badly it is now unreadable. The weathering was already in progress in the early twentieth century when Benjamin Franklin Wilbour transcribed it. He added several question marks to his transcription indicating the difficulty he had reading the stone, but he was able to decipher:

> Mary Daughter of Weston Soule and Sarah his wife.
> She died Sept 30, 1778 in her 3d year.

For more on Weston Soule's (also Sowle) descendants and their burying ground just over the wall to the southwest please see LC028 on page 77.

Captain Aaron Wilbor passed the northern portion of his farm to his son Thomas and the southern portion of the farm to his son Francis. In 1809 Francis sold the meadow containing the family burying ground to Charles Manchester, a distant relative by marriage, but reserved the burying ground for himself and his heirs. Job Tripp purchased the same meadow in 1834, and again the burying ground was reserved from the sale.

Since Job did not have the privilege of burying in the existing Wilbor lot, he created his own four-rod-square burying ground just to the east of the original one, most likely in 1851 when his wife Patience Earl Brownell Tripp died at the age of 68. Patience has two grave markers: a flat one that was probably installed around the time of her death and a large, upright double stone erected after Job died in 1880. Patience's flat stone is identical to the ones used for several neighbor women who died around the same time and are buried nearby in the Sowle Cemetery (LC028). There is only one other gravestone in the Tripp Lot. It is shared by Job and Patience's two young grandsons, William and Charles, who died in 1857 and 1863. They were the children of Job and Patience's daughter Patience and her husband Thomas Crosby.

Photo by Bart Brownell.

Thomas is credited with bringing a Malay rooster from a ship in New Bedford back to this farm. His brother-in-law William Tripp used it to develop the first Rhode Island Red chickens.

28

SOWLE BURYING GROUND

498 Long Highway
Gravestones dated 1822-1867.
This burying ground appears to be abandoned by the family.
Surrounded by private property. Private laneway.
Visitation by appointment only. Contact the Little Compton Historical Society
   at 401-635-4035 or lchistory@littlecompton.org.

Photo by Bart Brownell.

The members of the Sowle (also Soule) family buried here are connected by marriage to the Wilbors buried just to the north (LC027). Weston Sowle (1729-1825) married three times. His second wife Sarah Wilbor (1748-c.1802) was the daughter of Captain Aaron and Mary Wilbor. Weston was a seaman and had a reputation for great physical strength. At the end of his life he referred to himself as a gentleman, an indication that he had accumulated significant wealth. Weston and Sarah had at least one child, a daughter named Mary who died in 1778 in her third year and was buried in the Wilbor family lot with an inscribed gravestone that is no longer legible.

While he was married to Sarah, Weston appears to have had another family in Westport with a woman named Philena Manchester. Their son Hiram Sowle Manchester was born in 1774 and used both Manchester and Sowle as his last name in different documents. Weston eventually married Philena in 1803, we presume after Mary's death, though Mary has no surviving gravestone and no known death date. Weston and Philena lived in Westport. Their son Hiram died in 1822, and Weston died in 1825. In 1839, Hiram's son John Sowle was doing very well in Boston and established a business that would eventually become Doll & Richards, a respected fine art dealer. In the same year he purchased the southern part of what was once Captain Aaron Wilbor's Little Compton farm and lived there part-time.

His household included an amazing assortment of female relatives:

- His paternal grandmother Philena Sowle (1751-1846)
- His maternal grandmother Priscilla Earl (1749-1840)
- His mother Lydia Earl Sowle (1780-1852)
- His sister Anne Sowle (1806-1846)
- His wife Mary D. Wood Sowle (1810-1867)
- His mother-in-law Patience Wood (1777-1850)

Five of the six women, everyone except his wife Mary, died between 1840 and 1852 and were buried in this cemetery John and Mary created on their Little Compton farm diagonally across the wall from the Wilbor-Tripp Burying Grounds. Each woman was memorialized with an unusual, small marble gravestone lying horizontally on a small base of brown sandstone. The stones have not weathered well and are becoming difficult to read. Several are broken.

Patience Earl Brownell Tripp lived on the farm just to the north and is buried nearby in the Tripp Burying Ground with an identical gravestone. The similarity of the gravestones and the Earl surname suggest that Patience may have been related.

Example of one of the horizontal gravestones in the Sowle Burying Ground.

When Mary died in 1867, John provided her with a larger, more traditional gravestone that has fallen off its base but is in otherwise good condition today.

There are probably no men buried in this lot. Weston and Hiram Sowle died before John owned this property. Weston has no known surviving gravestone. Local historian Benjamin Franklin Wilbour recorded a gravestone for Hiram here in 1959 but it is no longer present. It may have been just a memorial stone. John Sowle has no known surviving gravestone, and his death date is not known.

29

THOMAS BROWNELL LOT

Maurolou Farm, 530 Long Highway
Gravestones dated 1800-1842, numerous fieldstones and numerous
  unmarked graves.
Privately owned.
Visitation by appointment only. Call Susan at 401-533-2156.

Unusual tales of death fascinated early Americans and were frequently published in newspapers. A story concerning this branch of Little Compton's large Brownell family appeared in the *New-England Palladium*, a Boston paper, in 1817.

DEATHS - At Little Compton,
23d ult. Mrs. Deborah
Manchester, consort of Mr.
Daniel Manchester, in the 33d
year of her age. Her infant child,
eight days after her departure,
as though exhaled by the
departed spirit of its affectionate
mother, took its flight from these
shores of mortality and distress,
to the bosom of its mother, aged
11 days. Also, on the 27th, Mrs.
Hannah Brownell, in the 59th
year of her age - being four days
after the death of her daughter,
Deborah Manchester – also on
the 3d inst. Mrs. Mary Brownell,
in the 98th year of her age. Thus
in the course of thirteen days, did
death make conquest over four
generations, all from one house,
and all in lineal descent, from
the eldest down to the infant.

Photo by Bart Brownell.

Of the four people mentioned in this newspaper story only Deborah Manchester has a surviving inscribed gravestone. This Brownell burying ground, one of four Brownell cemeteries in Little Compton, is an excellent example of the failure of inscribed gravestones to tell the full story of a cemetery or the people buried there.

As the only man with a surviving inscribed gravestone Thomas Brownell (c.1720-1808) seems to be a central figure here, and for many years this burying ground has been referred to as the Thomas Brownell lot. In fact, Thomas, who had no children, shared this burial ground with his brother Richard (1715-1780). It is Richard's wife Mary Wilbor (1719-1817) who is mentioned in the newspaper above, and the others in the story descend from them. Neither Richard nor Mary has a surviving gravestone. Thomas' wife Eunice Taylor (1728-1800) has the oldest dated stone in the lot. Thomas and Eunice had no children. A 1959 cemetery survey reported a stone belonging to Elias Brownell (1778-1838), the son of James Brownell and the grandson of Richard Brownell. That stone was no longer present in 2010 when the cemetery was photographed for the state database, but Elias' wife Hannah Palmer's (1777-1842) stone was still there.

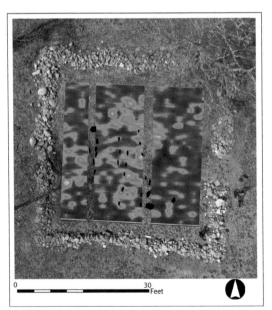

0   30 Feet

Ground penetrating radar courtesy of Professor Jon Marcoux, Salve Regina University.

There are a number of field-stones in this lot. Additionally, ground penetrating radar performed in 2018 revealed the presence of approximately a dozen completely unmarked graves. Though it looks rather empty today, almost every possible spot in this burying ground is occupied by a grave. This cemetery is probably much older than the 1800 date on Eunice's stone and may have been established by Thomas and Richard's father Captain Thomas Brownell (1679-1752). His wife Mary Crandall (1689-1732) was buried on the Commons twenty years before his death, but even though he was a prominent man, no surviving stone marks his final resting place.

Some of the graves marked with fieldstones, or now unmarked, certainly belong to Brownell family members. Others may be for their servants, like Mary Jamison (1736-1815) who worked for Thomas and Eunice Brownell for many years and remained a part of Thomas' nephew Richard's household after her employers' deaths. At least one grave may be for someone with no connection to the family at all. When Howard Huntoon sold this farm to Lou and Maureen Pieri in 1955 he shared the story of one of the people believed to be buried here:

> One night a traveling stranger knocked on the Brownells' door, asked for shelter for the night, and was provided with a room. The Brownells did not ask his name nor any other identifying information. In the morning, the stranger did not emerge from his room and the Brownells discovered that he had died during the night. With no way to return this man to his family or hometown, the Brownells buried him here.

As the farm passed from one generation to another, the Brownells did not provide their burying ground with any kind of protection in their numerous wills or deeds, but Lester Allen, one of the farm's twentieth-century owners, added a condition to its deed that the cemetery be preserved forever.

30
HENRY HEAD JR. LOT

Goosewing Farm, Long Highway
One gravestone dated 1755.
Burying ground reserved by the Head heirs per an 1812 deed, but now lost.
Private property. Private laneway.
No visitation.

The one surviving gravestone that makes up this historic burying ground was lost and found, then lost and found again.

From 1946 to 1990 the Wildes family farmed the land that once belonged to Henry Head Junior The Wildes siblings do not remember a cemetery on the property, now known as Goosewing Farm, but they do remember the day they discovered

Photo by Bart Brownell.

Photo by Bart Brownell.

Henry's gravestone face down in the bottom of a firepit. They rescued the intact stone and Meredith Wildes sketched it for a school project in the 1950s when she was about 13 years old.

Gravestone from an abandoned graveyard on a farm in Little Compton

Sketch by Meredith Wildes, c. 1956.

Twenty years later, Avila Moore and her brother Brent Junior were spending the summer on the farm when they rediscovered the gravestone, now broken. Avila and Brent were digging up a shark's head they had buried the summer before in order to harvest its teeth. Their shovel hit Henry's gravestone. The property owner, Eleanor Truesdale Marvell gave the stone to the Historical Society where it was stored for many years. Recently, Carl and Carol Acebes rein-stalled the stone at Goosewing Farm near where it was found and reunited it with its original footstone that was discovered against a wall in some brush.

Henry Head Junior was not the only Head family member buried on his farm. When Henry's grandson Benjamin sold the farm to Jonathan Peckham in 1812 he wrote, "except a piece of land containing three square rods for a burying place including the graves which are on said land at present, this to remain to the said Benjamin Head for the possession of a burying place for him and his heirs and assigns forever." We do not know how many graves there were, who was buried in them, or whether or not they had inscribed gravestones. We do know there was more than one grave. In the nineteenth century there were several reports of local farmers simply plowing up burying grounds that belonged to previous landowners. It is possible this was the case here.

To complicate matters even further, in the first half of the twentieth century someone on the farm told local historian Benjamin Franklin Wilbour that the burying ground was no more because all the bodies had been moved to the Union Cemetery. Many members of the Sisson family, the owners of the farm from 1853 to 1880, are buried in the Union Cemetery, but Town Council records do not record any requests to move the remains of Heads or Sissons, and the Union Cemetery records shed no light on the subject.

31
GIFFORD LOT

15 Albert Lane, off Old Harbor Road, Adamsville
Gravestones dated 1802-1822 and numerous fieldstones.
Owned by the Gifford heirs per John Gifford's 1840 deed.
The lot appears to have been abandoned by the family.
Surrounded by private property. Private laneway.
Visitation by appointment only. Call the Killenberg family at 919-360-9792.

The Gifford lot is a well-preserved family burying ground that likely dates back to Christopher and Deborah (Perry) Gifford's settlement in the area in the late-seventeenth century and the deaths of three of their children: an infant Christopher in 1689, a daughter Merribah in 1708, and Aubrey, Christopher's twin, who also died young.

The Gifford homestead farm passed from father to son for several generations: Christopher (1658-1748) to Enos (1693-1769) to Joseph (1742-1811) to Silvester (1778-1842) to Joseph P. (b. 1816) and the cemetery passed with it. There are only three inscribed stones. One is for Joseph (1742-1811) a farmer and a blacksmith. Another, dated 1822, is for Joseph's sixteen-year-old grandson David, the son of Silvester and his wife Rhoda Manchester. The third stone presents us with a bit of a mystery. It

Photo by Bart Brownell.

reads, "Amy daughter of Silvester Gifford died in August 1802, aged 21 years." This Amy does not fit any of the available genealogical information. One explanation is that Amy was actually the daughter of Joseph and Patience Gifford born in 1780, and that the gravestone carver made a mistake by putting her brother Silvester's name on both her stone and the stone for her nephew David. Amy and David's stones are similar and were probably carved at the same time. All three stones have a simple willow branch design that does not appear on other gravestones in Little Compton. There are also more than a dozen uninscribed gravestones in the lot marking the resting places of other Gifford family members.

The burying ground appears in the written record for the first time in 1840 when Silvester purchased a four-acre lot from his cousin John Gifford. John "excepted and reserved" the 25 square rod burying ground from the sale. Upon his death in 1842, Silvester divided his property equally between his two surviving sons, Joseph P. and Clark, but the following year the Little Compton Probate Court received a complaint against Clark from someone concerned that "for want of discretion in managing his estate he is likely to bring himself and his family to want and thereby render himself and his family chargeable to his town." To prevent Clark from requiring taxpayer support, the town appointed Ebenezer P. Church to be the guardian of his estate. Clark died three years later at age 25 leaving his young wife Mary Ann Tripp behind. The Gifford family sold the four-acre "Burying Ground Lot" which was part of Clark's inheritance, to Ebenezer P. Church in 1847, once again "excepting and reserving the burying ground situated on the north side of the above described premises containing about 25 rods of land also reserving a right to pass and repass to said burying ground through the above described lot." The burying ground occupied only a small portion of the four acres, the remainder was used for farming. There appears to have been no stone wall surrounding the graves, and there still is none today.

"The Gifford Place" has changed hands many times since Ebenezer Church acquired it, and with each sale the new property owners have continued to successfully preserve the burying place within its bounds.

32
GIFFORD LOT SOUTH

14 Albert Lane, Off Old Harbor Road, Adamsville
Fieldstones.
Surrounded by private property. Private laneway.
No visitation.

In 1994 when Peter and Stephanie Derbyshire purchased their new home, they had no idea it contained a burying ground. Their neighbor John Kneeland pointed out the overgrown area containing approximately eight fieldstone graves, and since then the Derbyshires have kept the area clear.

For many years this small burying ground was listed as "Unknown" by both the Little Compton Historical Society and the state. Reviewing the complicated chain of wills and deeds that pertain to the property shows that the land was part of the large Gifford family holdings. The burying ground likely contains Gifford family members. This burying ground is within view of the small Gifford lot to the north and is separated from it by a right of way. It is likely that this unknown lot and the Gifford Lot next door (LC031) were both originally contained within the Gifford's four-acre "Burying Ground Lot."

33, 37, 38

SAKONNET BURYING GROUNDS

John Dyer Road – Mullin Hill Road Area
Private property.
No visitation.

The Rhode Island Historical Cemetery Commission lists three burying grounds in Little Compton as "Indian" or "possibly Indian." A fourth is listed in a 1959 cemetery census.

The Sakonnet People lived in what we now call Little Compton and Acoaxet for thousands of years. A map made by Newport minister Ezra Stiles in 1760 indicates that there were 2,000 Sakonnets living here in 1670. People who identified as Sakonnet, like Sarah Howdee who died in 1827, lived in the community until the nineteenth century. In 1807 the Town Council voted to pay a reasonable sum for the coffin of Exy Sampson, an Indian woman. The record does not list where she was buried. No Native person has a known inscribed gravestone in Little Compton, but there must be tens of thousands of Sakonnet burials, dating both before and after the arrival of the English. They could be anywhere on the Sakonnet peninsula from the Sakonnet River to the West Branch of the Westport River, once called the Acoaxet River.

The traditional research techniques that we have used to learn more about the burying grounds of Little Compton's European settlers are ineffective when researching indigenous burying grounds. No primary sources - land evidence, probate or vital records - mention these places. Instead we have relied on secondary sources, oral histories and the historic landscape to try and identify and understand the town's Sakonnet Burying Grounds.

Most of those stories focus on a corner of land between John Dyer Road and Mullin Hill Road. After King Philip's War in 1676 about a dozen Sakonnet men and women owned land in the Adamsville and Acoaxet areas by virtue of an English-style deed. All of this land passed into English hands by about 1720. There are reliable reports of an Indian Meeting House with Native preachers on the east side of John Dyer Road. When this Meeting House disbanded is unknown, but it was active in 1741 when a newspaper story mentions its deacon, Jacob Hawney. We have heard

Photo by Bart Brownell.

from several sources that in the 1930s excavating work on John Dyer Road unearthed indigenous graves, and that the State Police had to step in to stop grave robbers. We have been unable to verify this story with newspaper articles or police reports. A long-time resident reported that the graves contained skeletons in the fetal position facing east, and that the remains were treated very disrespectfully by local youths. We have also been told by an Acoaxet resident that her father ran out with a rifle to protect the Indian burying ground on his property from potential grave robbers.

Life-long residents have grown up hearing about Little Compton's Indian burying grounds. A few people know where they are, but the history of disrespect these sacred places have endured has made us protective of them.

LC033, 37 and 38 are in the John Dyer Road – Mullin Hill Road area on private property.

An additional unnumbered burying ground is on the western side of Little Compton, north of Swamp Road, also on private property, and is said to contain the final resting place of seventeenth-century Sakonnets, including Awashonks who was the female Sachem of the Sakonnets in the 1670s. After King Philip's war, a small number of Awashonks' band were allowed by Plymouth officials to return to Little Compton in 1676 to an area called Three Quarter Miles Square, just south of Taylor's Lane. By 1681 this land was in English hands. In 1937 local historians reported that they were certain this was Awashonks' burial site and marked the Swamp Road location with a historic marker during Rhode Island's 300th anniversary celebrations. The marker is long gone and so is the gravel mound that once identified the gravesite.

34

WILLIAM & MARY WILBUR BURYING GROUND

100 East Main Road
Three gravestones dated 1806, 1818 and 1830.
Owned by the heirs of Samuel Wilbur per his 1844 will.
Accessed via private property.
Visitation by appointment only. Contact Pam Church at
  401-635-4641 or pamchurch@hotmail.com.

Photo by Bart Brownell.

William Wilbur (1721-1818) and his wife Mary Babcock Wilbur (1745-1806) have the places of honor in this small burying ground, close to its western wall. Their son Samuel (1758-1844) created the burying ground for them and attempted to preserve it for future family members, though it is unlikely that anyone used it after his death. Both its gravestones and the available historic records indicate that William, Mary and Samuel's daughter Elisabeth (1792-1833) are the only ones buried here. Probate documents tell us that their handsome matching gravestones were not installed until after Samuel's death in 1844. Purchasing these stones was Samuel's first concern in his will:

> First – I request my Executor to this my will to see that suitable Slate Grave Stones decently lettered, be set at my grave and also the grave of my First Wife and Daughter Betsey and also the Graves of my Father and Mother. My will further is that the Burying Ground on my Estate be kept for a Family Burying Ground and kept in good order with a Privilege to pass and repass to and from the same, also that the Grave Stones aforesaid be furnished in One year after my deceased and erected at their proper places at the Expense of my estate.

Samuel's friend Alexander Brownell served as his executor and ordered five, high-quality slate stones from a gravestone carver who marked his work "Warren F R." When the stones arrived three were installed here and two were brought to the Old Burying Ground on the Commons to mark Samuel's grave and that of his wife Charlotte Searle (1771-1799).

Many Little Compton graves sat unadorned for years, perhaps marked only by a simple fieldstone to spare the gravedigger any confusion in the future. Charlotte Searle's grave waited 45 years for its current gravestone. Samuel's mother Mary's grave waited 38 years for its carved stone. Benjamin Franklin Wilbour reports that Mary Wilbur died in Westerly. We do not know if her body was actually brought here for burial. If it was not, this would be a memorial stone rather than a gravestone. There is no gravestone for her in Westerly.

Unlike many early-nineteenth-century American men, Samuel did not remarry after his wife's death. Samuel refers to Charlotte as his "First Wife" in his will, but it is likely that he used that term in the way we would use "late wife" today. There are no records of a second marriage for Samuel, and at his death he did not list a second wife among his heirs. After Charlotte's death, Samuel and their young daughter Betsey (Elisabeth on her gravestone) probably lived with his parents. As Betsey grew she would have assumed more of the household responsibilities and would have kept house for her father after her grandmother's death in 1806, to the extent her own health allowed. Betsey died in 1830 at the age of 38.

At the end of Samuel's life, he was assisted by his housekeeper Ruth Palmer. Ruth and Samuel's younger brother Hezekiah were his only heirs, and Samuel divided his land equally between them. Even with her inheritance, Ruth struggled financially after Samuel's death and mortgaged the property on more than one occasion, finally losing it in 1851. Single women had limited options in the mid-nineteenth century and often found it difficult to earn a living especially as they aged. In 1850 a 72-year-old Ruth Palmer was living by herself in a room in the home of John Palmer in Pottersville. She has no known death date or gravestone.

35
TOMPKINS BURYING GROUND

South side of Tompkins Lane
No surviving gravestones.
Owned by the heirs of Nathaniel Tompkins per their 1854 deed.
Surrounded by private property.
No visitation.

Eighteen different deeds dated between 1854 and 1982 contain language meant to protect this family burying ground. All clearly identify it as belonging to Nathaniel Tompkins and his relatives. Unfortunately, while the memory of the burying ground was carefully preserved in the historic record, the space itself was fading away from the physical landscape.

The Tompkins Burying Ground was just a shadow when the current owner purchased the property in 1982. Someone had removed most of its wall stones leaving just a footprint in the Earth. According to a cemetery survey, the lot once contained two marble stones for Nathaniel Tompkins and Benjamin S. Pearce, but they were already gone by 1959. The few remaining slate gravestones had no inscriptions and had delaminated – splitting into layers like the pages of a book. They were unsalvageable. Since her purchase, the owner has reimagined the burying ground by having its walls rebuilt and by creating a perennial garden within its bounds.

Photo by Bart Brownell.

Like their burying ground, evidence of this branch of the Tompkins family has also faded through the years. As a working class, even poor family, they left less documentary evidence than many other Little Compton families. They did not write wills; they did not serve in elected positions, and they were overshadowed in the records by other more prosperous men also named Nathaniel Tompkins. Early map makers chose not to include their dwelling house on our local maps making them even harder to find. Still, enough evidence remains to begin to understand their lives.

Michael Tompkins (1722-1771) and his wife Sarah Dring (d. 1827) are perhaps the oldest family members buried here. At approximately 12 acres their homestead farm was smaller than most in Little Compton but had the unique feature of three cranberry bogs. A stone sluice leading to the bogs can still be seen today. Their son Nathaniel Tompkins (1756-1833), a private in the Revolution, inherited the farm. He and his wife Sarah Snell (1759-1837) suffered the loss of their 25-year-old son Michael, a fisherman, when he was murdered by Benjamin Snell, probably a relative of his mother's, in a dispute in 1806. A newspaper story states that Benjamin shot Michael in the bowels killing him immediately.

Toward the end of his life Nathaniel petitioned for his Revolutionary War pension submitting pages and pages of testimony tracing his three years of service in both the Rhode Island State Troops in Newport after the British occupation and in the Little Compton militia guarding the shore. Officials did not award the pension before Nathaniel's death in 1833. His widow took up the cause, submitting her own claim and writing:

> I had two children born after marriage and before the end of the war. After our marriage, when my husband was away in the service I had to do, and did, many things, out of doors, that women in this town think they cannot do. We suffered great privation at that time.

Neighbors testified that Sarah's single daughter Permilla was her sole source of support after Nathaniel's death and that the women lived in poverty. Sarah's pension request was successful. After Permilla's death in 1846 her brothers and sisters sold the property out of the family and, like so many Little Compton people, reserved the small burying ground for their perpetual use without ever burying there again.

Photo by Bart Brownell.

36

PERRY SIMMONS BURYING GROUND

11 Mullin Hill Road
One gravestone dated 1850 and fieldstones.
Owned by The Nature Conservancy.
Visitation by appointment only. Call the
*   Nature Conservancy at 401-331-7110.*
Refer to the Henry Manton Property.

A single inscribed gravestone, rising among the rough fieldstones evokes a sense of mystery in this lot. Inscribed stones in a family burying ground often provide context and offer clues for connecting the people buried there. But without that information we are left wondering who was Holder Reckords and why is he buried here? Who else is buried here, and what connects them?

Little Compton Families, a town-wide genealogy, tells us that Holder Reckords (also Records) (1817-1850) married Hannah Simmons (born c. 1820), the daughter of Perry and Lydia (Stoddard) Simmons in 1839. The 1850 Federal Census shows Holder and Hannah living next door to her parents in the home of James Taber. Holder was born in Westport and worked as a stonemason. Death records reveal that Holder drowned in 1850. Sadly, on at least one occasion the back of his gravestone has been used for target practice. The uninscribed stones surrounding Holder probably belong not to other members of the Reckords family, but to the Perry Simmons clan.

Perry Simmons and wife, Lydia Stoddard had four children: sons Perry Simmons Junior (1820-1878), Philip (1815-1881), and Brownell (b. 1817), and daughter Hannah Reckords Grinnell, who remarried after Holder's death. In her will Lydia instructs her son Perry, "to furnish my executor with the means to pay all my just debts and funeral expenses and erect or cause to be erected suitable grave stones at my grave." If Perry Junior purchased stones for Lydia, they do not survive today.

When Perry Simmons Junior died, his estate spent $25 for a coffin and other expenses, and $2.50 for grave digging. Lydia, Perry Senior, and Perry Junior probably account for three of the five to ten graves marked with uninscribed fieldstones.

Census records show that Lydia's elderly parents, Hannah Sawdy Stoddard (1764-c. 1835) and Brownell Stoddard (1756-1843) lived with the Simmons until their deaths. Brownell was a private in the Revolutionary War, and he received his pension checks at Perry Simmons' address. Perhaps Stoddard and Hannah are also buried in this lot.

In his will Perry Simmons Junior specifies that upon the death of his wife, Eliza Clarke Pierce Simmons (1839-after 1900), the family farm should pass to his step-daughter Ardelia Pierce (1855-after 1940). Ardelia and her husband Jesse Palmer lived on the farm until they sold it out of the family. From subsequent sales of the property, there is no sign that this cemetery was reserved for the family's future use or excluded from property transfers.

Careful historical research yields a picture of a multigenerational, blended family. But we can never know everything, and these gaps in knowledge open spaces for mystery to persist among the old graves.

Photo by Marjory O'Toole.

39

SIMMONS HILL
BURYING GROUND

Long Highway
No visible gravestones.
This lot is not currently maintained.
Private property.
No visitation.

This small, walled lot perched atop Simmons Hill has the look and feel of a burying ground, but there are no gravestones to help us identify the people buried here. There is, however, an abundance of historical evidence linking this burying ground to the Simmons family who, for generations, operated the grist mill at Simmons Pond to the east. Maps from 1850, 1870 and 1895 show that the property belonged first to William Simmons (1767-1853) and later to his grandson William T. Simmons (1825-1904).

William Simmons' 1854 probate records clearly identify a "Burying Ground Lot" adjacent to Long Highway and near the cart-way leading to the mill.

William Simmons and his wife Rebekah Soule (1771-1862) may be the last Simmons buried here. Their son Benjamin died in Fall River in 1842, and their grandson William T. Simmons, like many turn-of-the-twentieth-century Little Compton residents, chose to be buried in Pleasant View Cemetery in Tiverton.

William Simmons was the fifth generation of his family to live on this Long Highway farm, but we cannot assume that all of his ancestors are buried in this small lot. The first William Simmons (1672-1765) to live in Little Compton and his wife Abigail Church (1680-1720) buried at least three of their children in the Old Burying Ground on the Commons.

Abigail died at the age of 40 and is buried near her children on the Commons with a beautifully carved stone from the John Stevens Shop. William has no surviving gravestone. Their son, Captain Benjamin Simmans (spelling varies) (1713-1788) and his wife Mercy Taylor (1717-1796) are also buried on the Commons with handsomely carved gravestones. The next generation, Samuel Simmons (1742-1821) and Phebe Manchester Simmons (died before 1802), have no surviving gravestones and may be the first family members buried in this plot rather than the Old Burying Ground.

Photo by Letty Champion.

40

Constant & Susannah Seabury Burying Ground

Old Main Road, Windmill Hill
Two gravestones dated 1806 and 1816.
Privately owned.
No visitation.

The earliest Seaburys to live in Little Compton chose to be buried in the Old Burying Grounds on the Commons. Constant Seabury's parents and grandparents are all buried there. Constant (1749-1806) and his wife Susannah Gray Seabury (1751-1816) chose, instead, to be buried on their own farm with handsome slate gravestones and footstones. Susannah

Photo by Bart Brownell.

Seabury's headstone refers to her as the "relic" of her husband Constant. This term was commonly used in place of "widow" at that time.

Constant and Susannah may be the only ones buried here. Their son Robert inherited the property and its burying ground, but his wife Caroline Woodman (1789-1857) is buried in the old cemetery at the Old Stone Church. Robert's burial site is unknown.

In Little Compton, several other small family burying grounds, like the William and Mary Wilbur Burying Ground (LC034) and the Tripp Burying Ground (LC046), also came into use in the early 1800s and fell out of use just a few decades later as larger community cemeteries, like the Union Cemetery and Pleasant View in Tiverton, came into vogue.

Constant Seabury was a farmer and a tanner, just like his father Benjamin before him. Almost every family in early Little Compton farmed and did something else, a trade or a business to stay productive during the long winter days and to help make ends meet. Early Little Compton farms raised sheep for their wool, grew flax to produce linen, and kept cows, pigs and poultry for the family's own consumption and for sale. Any extra products – butter, cheese, salted meats, candles, lumber, barrel staves, and leather – were sold to merchants and placed on ships that traveled throughout the Atlantic world. When Constant died, his inventory of $145 in leather was by far the most valuable thing he owned besides his land and his home.

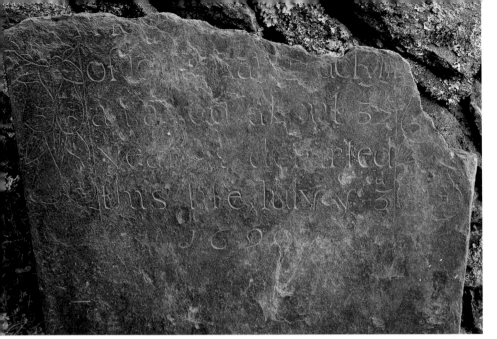

41
BLACKMAN BURYING GROUND

Misidentified

There is probably no Historic Cemetery 41 in Little Compton. A broken gravestone, most likely removed from the Old Burying Ground on the Commons, has led to the belief that a Blackman Burying Ground once existed on the northeast corner of West Main Road and Meeting House Lane. Sarah Soule Wilbour wrote in her diary about this partial gravestone belonging to Jonathan Blackman when it was discovered in the cellar of Follen Beebe's house in 1887. Eventually the stone found its way to the Little Compton Historical Society and is now a part of the permanent collection. Rhode Island law forbids individuals from possessing unearthed gravestones. They must either be returned to their original locations or held by a museum.

Surviving gravestones suggest that the Blackman family buried their dead in the Old Burying Ground on the Commons. Jonathan Blackman's mother, or perhaps step-mother, Sarah Blackman Jones was buried there in 1712 with a John Stevens hanging-toothed skull gravestone. Jonathan's son, also named Jonathan (1688-1717), and his daughter-in-law Mary Shaw (1689-1713) were buried on the Commons as well, both with John Stevens stones. Jonathan Senior was probably also buried on the Commons near these family members. At some point his gravestone broke and was taken to the nearby cellar where it served as a flat surface for a pork tub. Workmen discovered the gravestone shortly after Follen Beebe purchased the house, which had long been a Gray family farm.

Jonathan Senior's gravestone is interesting even in its broken state. It is inscribed 1690, making it the oldest dated gravestone in Little Compton. It is clear though, that it is not the oldest gravestone. John Stevens began carving here after his arrival in 1700. Jonathan's stone displays a type of italic lettering that John Stevens began using around 1713. It is very likely that Jonathan Junior ordered backdated gravestones for his father at the same time he ordered stones for his wife Mary after her death in 1713, and that both stones once stood near each other in the Old Burying Ground on the Commons.

42

Brightman Lot

Near 60 Quicksand Pond Road
Three gravestones dated 1817, 1822 and 1833.
Owned by heirs of Nathaniel Pearce per his 1852 deed.
Visitation during daylight hours.
Drive past the cemetery entrance and park on the grass.

The inscribed slate stone in this lot marks the grave of a woman who sidestepped misfortune.

Elizabeth "Betsey" Sisson of Tiverton (c. 1757-1822) bore three daughters out of wedlock. Most unwed mothers at the turn of the nineteenth century endured lives of poverty and instability. Shunned by polite society and often rejected by family, their children were frequently bound out to other people's households where they were vulnerable to exploitation. Yet Elizabeth Sisson lived a different version of unwed motherhood, working as the housekeeper for her daughters' father, John Almy of Tiverton (1764-1808). In his will, John claimed the girls as his own and bequeathed six hundred dollars to each of his "beloved daughters." He also left them a

farm in Westport and numerous household goods to share. In addition, John provided for the comfort and security of Elizabeth, to whom he referred in his will as "my now housekeeper."

When she died in 1822, Elizabeth "Betsey" Sisson was a woman of modest means with an estate worth $400. She was buried in the family burying ground on the Little Compton farm of her daughter and son-in-law Elizabeth and Lemuel Brightman. Her gravestone is inscribed:

> As you are now so I have been,
> As I am now so you wilst be.

Lemuel Brightman (1786-1862) inherited the farm upon his father Israel's death. Lemuel and Elizabeth (1794-1862) had seven children, six of whom survived childhood. Their

Photo by Bart Brownell.

deceased, unnamed infant (d.1817) appears to be the first person buried in the Brightman lot. They buried another son, Holder Brightman (c. 1812-1833), who died at age 21, leaving behind his 19-year-old widow Martha Chase (1814-1893).

When Lemuel sold the farm to Nathaniel Pearce in 1841, he didn't except or reserve the burial ground portion of the property. When Nathaniel sold the property eleven years later, the deed specified, "Reserving to myself three rods of land in the north end of the Burying Ground on said farm, and a privilege to pass and repass to and from the same." But as far as we can tell, Elizabeth Sisson and her two grandsons are the only people buried here.

43
SAWYER BURYING GROUND

Corner of Oak Forest Drive and Sakonnet Trail
Fieldstones.
Owned by the heirs of Lemuel Sawyer II per an 1870 deed to Asa Davol.
This cemetery appears to be abandoned by the family.
Roadside parking.

This small lot survived the 1980s creation of the Oak Forest subdivision as an overgrown tangle of briars and brush. A neighborhood "old timer" referred to it as an "Indian Burying Ground" because it had no inscribed stones. That inaccurate label might have stuck forever,
if not for the efforts of other neighbors.

Claire Johnson and her daughter Kate Johnson, PhD, spotted what they believed to be a fieldstone marker in the lot while walking by one day. The Johnsons shared the cost of clearing the burying ground with Dan and Lynn Sullivan, revealing three small headstones and two footstones all made of simple uninscribed fieldstone. Claire discovered that the cemetery had been registered with the state as Historical Cemetery 43 (LC043) in 1978. The Oak Forest Homeowners

Photo by Bart Brownell.

Association purchased an official sign, and Steve Johnson hung it on a nearby oak.

Claire recruited another Oak Forest neighbor, Bob Harvey, Scoutmaster for Little Compton Boy Scout Troop 29 for additional help. Under Bob's guidance Zachary Eddy adopted the cemetery as his Eagle Scout project and recruited other Scouts and their parents to rebuild the burying ground's stone walls, remove saplings and rake and remove leaves.

At the same time, Kate Johnson, an archeologist, conducted deed and other historical research connecting the cemetery to the Sawyer family. The 60 acres that now make up the Oak Forest development were once Lots 32 and 33 in the 1678 division of 30-acre lots in Little Compton. By 1789

Zachary Eddy during clean up.
Photo courtesy of Claire Johnson.

John and Josiah Sawyer owned the 60-acre farm that bounded the "Spruce Swamp" to the northeast. They sold the farm to their brother Lemuel I in 1793, and after his death it eventually passed to his youngest son Lemuel II. Lemuel II and his wife Abby Manchester sold the farm out of the family to Asa Davol in 1870 and, like so many local land-owners, made a special effort to preserve their family burying ground for their use and for their descendants by reserving the lot from the sale of the farm and by claiming the right to pass and repass to it forever.

Though the Sawyer family no longer maintains, or perhaps even remembers, this small burial ground, their farm's most recent residents have joined together to ensure its preservation.

44
GREENE FAMILY CEMETERY

Colebrook Road
Privately Owned.
No visitation.

In the 1970s the Greene family received permission from the Town Council to establish this small cemetery on their private property for their family's use. As of 2018 the cemetery was unused.

45
MANLEY BURYING GROUND

30 Rockbridge Road
One gravestone dated 1868 and fieldstones.
Owned by the heirs of William Manley per his 1841 will.
Visitation during daylight hours.
Roadside parking.

Appearing before the Town Council in June 1877, Sylvester Cooley Manley requested and was granted permission "to remove bodies of his father and other friends to Westport." If Sylvester offered the reasons for his request, the Town Clerk taking minutes at that meeting did not record them.

Sylvester's great-grandmother, Temperence Turner Manley (1737–1804) purchased three adjacent lots in Little Compton and Westport between 1792 and 1795 and created a 100+ acre farm along the eastern shore of Quicksand Pond for herself, her only child William and his growing family. Temperence was a widow and so could purchase and own property at a time when married women could not.

The Manleys thrived on Temperence's farm. William (1767–1842) and his second wife Judith Snell (1769–1849) had two sons and five daughters. Their eldest son John (1790–1845) and his wife Bethany Brightman had

nine children. Their second son William Moore Manley (1796–1861) and his wife Abigail Brownell had seventeen children (including four sets of twins!). When Temperence died in 1804, she was likely buried here.

Temperence's will directed William to divide the farm between his sons John Manley and William Moore Manley. He did so using his own will in 1841. The family burying ground fell within the boundaries of John's 40-acre lot, so William ensured William Moore's family could use it as well:

> Excepting however a privilege to William M Manley to pass and repass the usual way through said John Manley's portion of said estate, also a privilege to said William M Manley and relatives to bury their dead when they choose in the Burying Place on said John Manley's portion of said estate

The single inscribed marble gravestone here marks the grave of Ruth Manley Head (1800–1868), William and Judith's youngest child. Palmer Head, Ruth's husband of fifty years, had Ruth buried here with her family of origin. He is buried in the Henry Head Senior Burying Ground on Maple Avenue. In his will, Palmer instructed his heirs to erect "suitable grave stones for me and my wife as soon after my decease as may be." Ruth's grave may have been either unmarked or marked by fieldstones between her death in 1868 and her husband's death in 1872.

According to Sylvester's petition to the Town Council, his father William Moore Manley was buried here before being moved to Beech Grove Cemetery in Westport, Massachusetts. The others moved to Beech Grove Cemetery may include some or all of Sylvester's siblings who died prior to 1877 and who have inscribed stones at Beech Grove today: Charles Manley, Daniel Manley, Oliver P. Manley (the second son given that name) and Susan A. Manley.

At least five fieldstone head- and footstone pairs remain at the Manley Burying Ground. In addition to Temperence Turner Manley, candidates for others buried here with uninscribed stones include:

- Temperence's son William Manley and his wife Judith Snell.
- Temperence's grandson John Manley and one or both of John's wives, Bethany Brightman Manley and Promillee Palmer Manley.
- Temperence's great-grandchildren, the three young children of William Moore and Abigail Manley who do not have inscribed stones at Beech Grove Cemetery: Oliver Perry Manley (the first child given that name), Abigail Manley and an unnamed infant

46
TRIPP BURYING GROUND

16 Long Highway
Gravestones dated 1833-1886 and fieldstones.
Privately owned. Surrounded by private property.
Visitation by appointment only. Call 401-635-0193.

This small family plot contains the inscribed gravestones of Abial and Phebe Tripp and five of their seven adult children. The Tripps bought the 30-acre tract straddling the boundary between Tiverton and Little Compton in 1809 from the Manchester family and made it their home. In 1833, the Tripp's 25-year-old daughter Sarah was the first family member to be buried here with an inscribed gravestone. Later that year her 28-year-old brother Abel became the second when he succumbed to a long illness. Father Abial and daughter Susan followed in 1834; four deaths for the family in just two years.

For many years the unwalled burying ground sat in the middle of a meadow and would have been visible to passersby on Long Highway. Unmarried daughter Mary lived on the farm after her parents' deaths and appears to be the last person buried there. Mary wrote her will 13 years before she died in 1886. Her very first item was, "I direct my body to be interred in the Tripp burying ground near where I live, and that my Executrix hereafter named shall procure and erect or cause to be erected suitable gravestones on or near the spot where my body shall be interred." Many nineteenth-century residents took their burials and their gravestones very seriously and left specific directions for them in their wills.

The farm and its meadow cemetery stayed in the Tripp family for several more generations until 1924 when Phebe Tripp Carr Millard sold the burying ground to Manuel and Lillian Ferreria. Phebe required "said Manuel Ferreria to build and maintain a wall around the Cemetery on said farm." Today the cemetery remains walled on two sides. This is one of the very few family cemeteries in Little Compton that was not reserved from the sale when the owners sold their farm out of the family. This means that the current property owner actually owns the cemetery as well as the surrounding property.

Though it seems that the Tripp Burying Ground was in use for just over 50 years, there are several rows of fieldstones to the east of the inscribed stones that appear to be gravestones for unknown individuals. It is possible the graves predate the Tripps, or they may mark the graves of other family members or servants.

47
STODDARD BURYING GROUND

Off Mullin Hill Road
One undated footstone and fieldstones.
Owned by Thomas Stoddard's heirs per his 1828 will.
This lot appears to have been abandoned by the family.
Surrounded by private property. Private laneway.
No visitation.

If gravestones embody the weight of loss, the stones in this lot are too small.

The threat of death was constant for American families throughout the eighteenth and nineteenth centuries. Nathaniel and Emlin (Wilbore) Stoddard were hit harder than most when their first four children died in the seven weeks between November 4, 1756 and December 31, 1756: Hannah, age four; Lydia, age two; Emlin, age one; and Joseph, an infant. All are likely buried here. An aptly-named fifth child, Comfort was born ten months after Emlin and Nathaniel's crushing loss. Later, four more daughters and a son joined the family: Susannah, Elizabeth, Martha, Ruth and Thomas.

Thomas Stoddard (1770-1828) married Sarah Wood. Growing up with five older sisters probably provided him with experiences and insights that guided him as the

Photo by Bart Brownell.

father of their five daughters: Christianna, Phoebe, Hannah, Betsey, and Metilda.

When Thomas reserved this burying ground on the family homestead in 1828 his father, mother, the four siblings who died in 1756, and a fifth sibling, Elizabeth (1763-1765) may already have been buried here. Deeding an easement to his fifth and youngest daughter Metilda, he reserved not just his wife's and daughters' rights to bury here, but his sisters' as well.

> the said lot of land to be kept forever, hereafter, for the sole purpose of a Buring Place, for myself my wife my children their heirs forever from generation to generation, also for my sisters, & their children, and grand children, and so on without end so long as their shall be room sufficient for purpose aforesaid; they having a right to pass to and from said premises at all times across my land when death may require it, doing as little damage as may be.

There is a poignancy to his phrase, "so long as there shall be room sufficient for purpose aforesaid," as if Thomas anticipated future burials threatening to tumble the walls of the three-rod square lot. Or perhaps Thomas was acknowledging that the lot was already near capacity, which is likely when we consider the possible burials here.

If the instructions in Thomas' will were followed, he and Sarah are buried here though there are no inscribed stones for them. Little Compton resident Charles Simmons remembers seeing several "Stoddard" stones here when he was young, but they were not reported when the cemetery was surveyed in 1959. The single remaining inscribed stone, a marble footstone bearing the initials "HS," probably belongs to Thomas and Sarah's daughter Hannah Stoddard (b. 1802). Thomas' parents and their five children who did not survive childhood may be here, as may Thomas' two unmarried sisters. Of his three married sisters, Susannah Stoddard Pearce alone has a known gravestone with her husband Isaac Pearce in Old Burying Ground on the Commons.

In this isolated lot, the single inscribed stone and handful of fieldstones seem inadequate – literally and figuratively – to account for the deaths in the Stoddard family.

48
SAMUEL CHURCH LOT

Old Harbor Road
Two gravestones both dated 1816.
Privately owned.
No public visitation.

Adamsville's Samuel Church was well on the way to becoming one of Little Compton's leading merchants when he died while making repairs to his new mansion house in 1816. Samuel came to Little Compton from New Bedford as a young man and invested heavily in Adamsville businesses. He opened a store, became Little Compton's first postmaster, owned a portion of the Adamsville mill, established a saltworks on the West Branch of the Westport River, and was part owner of a wharf and store at Westport Point, the sloop *Lydia*, and a distillery.

In 1803 he married Elizabeth "Betsey" Brownell and together they had six children. The couple began building a mansion house in 1815 at the corner of Adamsville Road and Old Harbor Road that still stands today. That September, The Great Gale of 1815 damaged much of the Churches' property including their unfinished home. Samuel died in April of 1816, reportedly when a beam fell on him during repairs. He was 35 years old.

Photo by Melinda Green.

Betsey, according to the custom of the times, inherited one third of her husband's estate while her children inherited the other two thirds. Betsey served as the estate administrator and oversaw all of her family's affairs including the completion of the mansion house and an addition to the family store. One of her first responsibilities as the new head of the family was to select a proper resting place for her husband. She chose to create a new family lot in the southwest corner of their property and erected a handsome set of slate stones honoring Samuel. Seven months later she had to do the same for her 17-month-old son, Philander.

Samuel and Philander are very likely the only two people buried in the Samuel Church Lot. Betsey married Pardon Brown of Little Compton in 1819, and the couple moved to Connecticut with her children. They sold their Little Compton and Westport property over the course of several years to a number of people. The town selected William A. Brown to act as the guardian of the children's estate and oversee the sale of their property. Those early deeds mention the cemetery in the boundary description of a half-acre house lot facing Old Harbor Road.

When the current owner of that house lot arrived in Little Compton about 50 years ago, the Church burying ground was no more. Someone had removed the two headstones and the two footstones and left them laying on the ground face-up, near the back wall of the house. They have been there ever since.

49

UNKNOWN

John Dyer Road – Mullin Hill Road
Private property.
No visitation.

There are reports of a single gravestone, or perhaps footstone, with initials carved in it, possibly "MP" or "WP." More research is necessary.

Photo by Bart Brownell.

50

WHITE FAMILY BURYING GROUND

North side of Bay Farm Lane, off West Main Road
Two fieldstones.
Owned by the heirs of Christopher T. White per an 1856 deed.
Private lane.
No visitation.

Today this small lot contains only two uninscribed fieldstones. It has been owned by members of the White family since 1751. The Whites descend from two Mayflower passengers, Francis Cooke and Peregrine White. Peregrine is known in Colonial history as the child born on the Mayflower in Cape Cod Harbor in 1620. Peregrine's great-grandson Christopher White, a blacksmith, moved from his parents' home in Dartmouth to Little Compton around 1739 when he married a local woman, Elizabeth Thurston. The couple eventually settled on a 60-acre portion of the Thurston Farm spanning both sides of the Great West Road and stretching to the Sakonnet River. Elizabeth's parents, Jonathan and Sarah Thurston arrived in Little Compton among the first English settlers and recorded their son Edward's birth here in 1679. The burying ground may be the final resting place for several generations of both Thurstons and Whites.

The farm passed from Christopher White to his son Thomas White and then to Thomas' grandson Christopher T. White who sold the farm to Oliver C. Brownell in 1856 "excepting and reserving" the rights to the family burying ground. Oliver immediately resold the farm to John C. G. Brown of Newport and once again reserved the burying ground for the White family.

It is unlikely that anyone has been buried in the family lot since Christopher T. White, a Civil War veteran, sold it and moved to Newport. The Union Cemetery was established on the Commons by this time and members of the White family began to be buried there. Even Simeon Wonderly, a farm-hand who worked for three generations of the White family, was buried in Row 1 of the Old Burying Ground on the Commons with a handsome marble stone when he passed away in 1881. Twentieth-century deeds for the property still reserve the cemetery for the use of Christopher T. White and his family.

51

DYER BURYING GROUND

Off John Dyer Road
No visible gravestones.
Owned by the heirs of John Dyer per his 1846 will.
Not maintained. Surrounded by private property.
No visitation.

This burying ground has been added to the list of Little Compton's historic cemeteries as a result of the *Remember Me* project.

John Dyer (1765-1846) owned property in both Westport and Little Compton and is often referred to as "John Dyer of Westport" in official documents. He refers to "the burying ground on my farm" in his 1846 will. An 1850 map of Little Compton shows the location of the farm he shared with his first and second wives Christian Brightman (1773-1826)

Photo by Bart Brownell.

and Mercy Lake (1799-1874). It also shows that the road now known as John Dyer Road, but referred to then simply as "the highway," took several sharp turns near the Dyer house. The burying ground is near one of these turns. Since 1850 the road has been straightened and the old road blocked. The remnants of the burying ground are now in the woods.

Local historian Benjamin Franklin Wilbour listed many of the members of John Dyer's family as being buried in either the old or new cemeteries near the Old Stone Church in Tiverton, so it is not clear who may be buried here. In his will John reserved the right for his family to use the burying ground forever. B.F. Wilbour did not include this cemetery in his 1959 list of burying grounds with inscribed stones.

Tercentenary by Molly Luce. Courtesy of the Currier Museum of Art.

LOST BURYING GROUNDS

A number of Little Compton burying grounds have been lost, either through the well-intentioned efforts of descendants to relocate them, the ill-intentioned efforts of others to erase them, or the natural effects of time and nature.

The Little Family Burying Ground

In 1877 an unnamed Little Compton resident wrote this scathing letter to the *New Bedford Standard*:

> *To the Editor of the Standard*
>
> *Quite a sensation has been caused by the fact that a large landholder in town, who inherited a portion of the Little farm, so called, through the purchase of his father, a member of the Society of Friends, has clandestinely desecrated the Little Burying Ground by removing the gravestones, ploughing up and planting with corn, not leaving a vestage of a grave or stone to mark the repose of the dead. The late Judge Fobes Little has now living no less than ten grandchildren to witness this*

transaction. Three of them live in New Bedford. In every transfer of the Little Estate this burying lot was reserved as shown by the records of the town. Unless the matter is speedily adjusted, law proceedings are probable.

There are just enough clues in this article to determine that the author was Phillip F. Little, better known locally as P.F. Little, a printing shop owner and a frequent contributor of Little Compton news to the New Bedford paper. Little was accusing Edward Howland, Little Compton's "Last Quaker," of the desecration. Edward's father, John B. Howland purchased the Fobes Little homestead on West Main Road from P.F. Little in 1850, and Edward inherited it upon his father's death in 1871. In the deed, P.F. Little specifically excluded the burying ground from the sale, meaning that the Howlands did not own it and should not have disturbed it in any way. Judge Fobes Little's probate accounts show that his executor purchased inscribed gravestones for him. It is very likely that these gravestones were among the ones removed. Though P.F. Little threatened to take Edward Howland to court, nothing seems to have come of it. There is no Little Burying Ground today, and Fobes Little's gravestones do not survive in any other Rhode Island cemetery.

Eseck Carr's Burying Ground

Eseck Carr, a cooper, lived on the west side of Willow Avenue in the early eighteenth century. When he died in 1744 he gave his whole estate to his only surviving son Robert, "excepting my Burying Place where I have buryed my dead near my dwelling house." At this time Eseck's dead included at least his wife Susanna, their daughter Martha who appears to have died in childhood and their son Eseck who died in 1728 at the age of 35. The Carrs were slave holders, and this burying ground may also have contained the remains of people enslaved in their household.

Eseck Senior was very specific about his wishes for the burying ground and wrote:

concerning which my will further is that my son Robert Carr as soon as conveniently he can erect a handsome stone wall about those graves, a quarter of an acre of land to lye for a perpetual burying place for my children and children's children, proven that shall so cause to make such use of it, and I also reserve for ye liberty to pass and repass to and from said burying place as they may have occasion.

When Robert sold the Carr family farm to Samuel Gray in 1766, he excepted and reserved for himself and his family "for ever a yard walled to ye west of my house containing 36 square rods for a burying place." Thirty-six square rods equals .225 acres. Two years later when Samuel Gray sold to Captain David Hillard, he also respectfully and correctly excluded the walled cemetery from the sale confirming that it was reserved for the use of the Carr family.

Robert Carr died in 1767; a newspaper story reported that he froze to death in the street. Robert's son William, who lived just north of his father, was brutally murdered in a cellar by his deranged son in 1810. These two men who died so tragically as well as other Carr family members were probably buried in the family lot after the farm was sold out of the family as they do not have surviving gravestones elsewhere. The Carr farm stayed in the Hillard family for three generations and was sold sometime before 1870 to John Clarke Gardiner Brown who lived there until 1914 when he sold the property to Cora Allen with a deed that reserved "the burying ground in the garden."

As the Willow Avenue Carrs died or moved away, their cemetery began to fade from the landscape. In the mid-twentieth century the language that once so carefully protected the burying ground disappeared from the town's deeds and wills. The Carr family burying ground is somewhere on their homestead farm, now known as the Holly Meadows neighborhood, but no living person knows its exact location. The frequent use of simple fieldstones as grave makers in Little Compton has made it especially easy for later landowners to overlook and repurpose small burying grounds either intentionally or accidentally.

The Town Farm Burying Ground

A newborn's death record provides strong evidence of a lost burying ground at the site of the former Town Farm on Grange Avenue. In 1842 the Town Council granted the Overseer of the Poor discretion to bury the town's poor at the asylum. No records of the various Keepers' decisions regarding the inmates' places of burial survive, with the exception of this one child's death record.

The town purchased the farm on Grange Avenue that became the town's poor farm in 1832. The Keeper of the Town Farm and his wife ran the farming operation and provided room and board to the residents who were either poor or disabled. In exchange, residents labored on the farm according to their abilities. A 1901 report describes its later years:

One and one-half story wooden house; heating by stoves; seven sleeping rooms with seven beds in good condition; board the town poor at the rate of three dollars per week

The single documented burial on the Town Farm shows that Male Baby Mersey survived three days in August 1918. He was the son of Edward and Ella (Davis) Mersey. His parents met each other at the Town Farm where she was the Keeper Adelbert Davis' daughter, and he was a hired hand. Baby Mersey's grandparents Adlebert and Florence Davis and his parents Edward and Ella are all buried in the Old Burying Ground on the Commons.

The Town Farm remained in operation for just over 100 years. Census records, Town Council records and Town Farm ledgers provide the names of fifty residents. The total number of residents over the course of those hundred years is unknown. The records document the deaths of twenty-nine people associated with the Town Farm. Ten of them are named; nineteen are not. Their places of burial are not known but would have likely been the Old Burying Ground on the Commons or the lost burying area on the Town Farm. See page 132 for the named residents.

The Taylor Lot

For reasons now unknown, Sarah Soule Wilbour, a nineteenth-century local historian with a keen interest in the town's historic cemeteries, moved the eighteenth-century gravestones of the Robert Taylor family from their small burying ground on Taylor's Lane to the Old Burying Ground on the Commons. They can be seen in Row 14, placed much closer together than many of the other stones in the cemetery. We do not know if the bodies of the deceased were moved as well. The tight placement of the gravestones indicates they were not. At the very end of the nineteenth century, there were numerous requests to the Town Council to move bodies in the community. None of these requests mention Taylor family members.

Blackman, Peckham, Gould

There has long been discussion of cemeteries by these names in Little Compton. Recent research indicates that they may not really exist. We will continue to investigate and welcome your input.

LC041   Blackman: Please see page 99.

LC210   John Gould's Burying Ground has been listed as "not yet found" in Little Compton. No one named John Gould ever owned land in Little Compton. We believe that all historic references to the Gould Burying Ground are actually referring to the John Gould Lot in Middletown (MT037).

LC600   Peckham family tradition suggests there was a burying ground on their first homestead farm in Little Compton, but Quaker records state:

> John Packhom of Seaconnet aged, he departed this lif at his own house in Seaconnet, the 4 day of ye 10 month 1722 and was bureyed in Friends bureying place near the meeting house in Seaconnet.

Based on the available evidence, we do not believe there was a separate Peckham burying ground in Little Compton.

Lost & Found

For more on burying grounds that have been lost and found please see:

We welcome information concerning other possible burying grounds in Little Compton. Please contact the Historical Society at 401-635-4035 or lchistory@littlecompton.org if you have information to share.

Bartholomen Hunt's gravestone by John Stevens I, 1717/18, Old Burying Ground on the Commons. Photo by Bart Brownell.

Little Compton & The John Stevens Shop

From crude skulls scratched into slate in the early 1700s to portrait stones skillfully carved in the 1770s, John Stevens, his sons, his apprentices, and his grandson held a near monopoly on Little Compton's carved gravestones for most of the eighteenth century.

John Stevens left England and landed in Boston in 1700. He soon made his way to Little Compton and sought shelter at Simon Rouse's tavern on the Great West Road, just north of the Quaker Meeting House. Stevens may have planned to stay for just a short while before taking a ferry across the Sakonnet River to Newport, a much more promising spot for a stonemason to find work. Instead, he lingered in Little Compton long enough to attract the attention of Marcy Rouse, the tavern-keeper's daughter. The two were married on January 1, 1701/02. John was fifty-five years old, and Marcy was twenty-three. The first half of John Stevens' life remains a mystery, but at an age when many of his contemporaries were becoming grandfathers, Stevens began a new chapter of his life with a young bride, no property of his own, and soon seven children.

With Stevens' arrival in Little Compton, community burial practices began to change from the universal use of uninscribed fieldstones to mark graves (or perhaps no permanent marker at all) to the occasional use of inscribed headstones and footstones by a small portion of the population. During his first decade in the area, Stevens produced just one or two carved

John Price's Gravestone, 1703, is likely the first inscribed stone in the Old Burying Ground on the Little Compton Commons. Photo by Letty Champion.

Detail: John Stevens' hanging-toothed skull. Photo by Marjory O'Toole.

William Pabodie's 1707 gravestone displays even text. Photo by Bart Brownell.

gravestones for Little Compton families each year.

A number of Stevens' early stones were for his wife Marcy's relatives. The very first stone Stevens carved may have been for John Price, Junior, the firstborn child of Marcy's cousin John Price and his wife Martha. The infant was only eighteen-days old when he died. The stone John Stevens made for the infant Price established a pattern of imagery and text that Stevens followed religiously for the next decade. The Prices later purchased (or were given) two more sets of grave-stones from Stevens memorializing their mothers Mary Price, Marcy's aunt who died in 1698, and Martha Graves, who died in 1700. Both sets were carved sometime after Stevens' arrival in Little Compton and were backdated to display the years the women died.

John Stevens was neither an artist nor a skilled stone cutter when he chiseled the text and scratched his simple designs into John Price's slate. Stevens may have been moved by the grief of the young parents, or by a request from his new family, when he applied his masonry skills to grave-stone carving for the first time. Stevens' winged design, called the "hanging-toothed skull" by gravestone scholars, is a simple version of the death's head icon often found on English and New England gravestones from this time. The uneven quality of the text on John Price's stone distinguishes it from Stevens' later gravestones, which display a clean, straight, typeset quality very different from this early attempt.

Stevens settled in Newport, where his main source of income was stone-masonry. The extensive Stevens family ledger books (owned by the Benson family, who run the John Stevens Shop today) show that he installed cooking areas on ships, paved yards, built chimneys, whitewashed, plastered, cut hearths and steps, dug and built cellars, and occasionally carved gravestones.

Steven's gravestones from this early period reflect a sense of sameness and stability, always on black slate, with the same simple death's head, etched rather than carved, and with block lettering. In 1711/12 Little Compton experienced an epidemic that claimed approximately twenty lives. Six of John and Mary Wood's children died between March 8 and March 16. The Woods and other Little Compton families ordered a total of fourteen gravestones for those who died that year, seven times the number of Little Compton gravestone orders Stevens received in any previous year. All of these stones featured his typical design.

As he approached his seventies, important changes took place for Stevens. He graduated from what was essentially a journeyman, working primarily by himself for customers, to a master, supervising experienced workers and overseeing the education of his sons in a larger business that included more frequent stone carving. Because he started his family so late in life, preparing at least one son to provide for the family after his death was urgent business. The logical choice was his oldest son John II, who was working with his father by the age of ten.

A few ledger records reflect these developments, but the changes are even more apparent in the gravestones produced by John Stevens and his workers during this 1713-1720 transitional period. Stevens began to work with new and talented people whose influence is clearly reflected in the stones the Stevens Shop began to produce. In 1714 Stevens' uniform block text began to incorporate upper and lowercase letters for the first time and then soon transitioned to a new more fluid italic style of lettering. (See Judith Peabodie's stone.)

Vincent Luti, an expert on the Stevens stonecarvers, believes that a

Judith Peabodie's 1714 gravestone features Stevens' hanging-toothed skull and a new form of italic lettering. Old Burying Ground on the Commons. Photo by Letty Champion.

John Dye's Gravestone, 1716, shows John Stevens' transition from a grinning skull to a pointy-chinned angel. Old Burying Ground on the Commons. Photo by Bart Brownell.

Pointy-chinned angel design attributed to an elderly John Stevens I. Photo by Bart Brownell.

Early moon-faced angel attributed to John Stevens II, c. 1720. Photo by Letty Champion.

new master carver, the "Boston Master," arrived in Newport around this time and that both the thirteen-year-old John II and the seventy-year old John I studied with him. As a result, both father and son underwent an awkward "apprenticeship" period producing some crude transitional stones, (see John Dye's stone.) and then emerged as master carvers with their own distinct angel designs. The first new design, a pointy-chinned angel, appears around 1716 and is attributed by Luti to John I. The second, a moon-faced angel appears around 1720, and was probably the work of John II.

Little Compton adopted these new angel designs earlier than many other New England communities for reasons both practical – it was what their stone carver offered – and emotional. The 1711/12 epidemic was a trying time for the people of Little Compton. Stevens too was grieving. He lost an infant daughter in 1710 shortly before the epidemic and an infant son in 1713 shortly after it. In the years following the epidemic, both carver and purchasers may have been happy to put the death's head's somber reminder of mortality behind them in exchange for the angel's more positive message of hope and salvation. This change in gravestone designs is often attributed to changes in religious thought brought about by the Great Awakening in the 1740s, but in Little Compton it occurred 20-25 years earlier, and is much more likely a result of the changes in John Stevens Shop than any religious movement.

The pointy-chinned angel stones stop appearing in Little Compton in 1720 (and in Newport in 1724) when John I transferred the business to John II and essentially retired. John II started carving moon-faced angels very naively around 1717 when he was just fifteen years old, but his designs improved quickly. By 1720 they were charming, and by 1725 they were quite elegant. Now a master himself, John II took charge of his younger brother William's apprenticeship, and by 1729 the nineteen-year-old William was producing his own stones very similar in style to his brother's. (See Dudley Davenport's stone.) The 1720s were a period of collaboration in the Stevens Shop when more than one man or boy may have worked on the same stone. As John I stepped back from the business his influence on his sons' work faded, and their carved text changed once again to a less italic, straighter, upper and lower-case style. John Stevens I passed away shortly before his ninetieth birthday in 1736. His sons carved his gravestone.

John Bull, a young man who had an unhappy apprenticeship in the Stevens Shop, ran away, and later operated a competing stone carving business in Newport, has a number of distinctive stones in Little Compton.

Late moon-faced angel attributed to John Stevens II, c. 1725. Photo by Letty Champion.

Dudley Davenport, 1732, Little Compton, attributed to William Stevens. Photo by Letty Champion.

John Steven's gravestone carved by his sons, 1736, Newport. Photo by Letty Champion.

Cynthia Searl gravestone by John Bull, 1784, Old Burying Ground on the Commons. Photo by Bart Brownell.

Constant Woodman's gravestone by John Bull, 1780. Woodman Lot East. Photo by Marjory O'Toole.

Badly-weathered portrait stone by John Stevens III for Ruth Church and her infant Mary, 1771. Photo by Marjory O'Toole.

Throop stones often feature long necks. Photo by Letty Champion.

John II's son, also named John, carried on the family tradition of stone carving and achieved a level of expertise that enabled him to create portrait stones that are considered historical treasures today. Though he was the third John Stevens, he frequently signed his stones John Stevens Jr.

During the Revolution and the British occupation of Newport, Little Compton residents could no longer do business with the Stevens and turned to other shops like the Throops of Bristol for their gravestones. As the eighteenth century drew to a close, gravestone styles in New England changed once again, from winged angels on slate to neoclassical urn and willow designs on marble. At this time Little Compton residents had many more gravestone carvers from whom to choose, and the carvers offered an ever-widening variety of styles.

Urn design on Isaac Bailey's 1813 gravestone. Old Burying Ground on the Commons. Photo by Bart Brownell.

For More on The Stevens Shop and New England Gravestones

Luti, Vincent. *Mallet & Chisel, Gravestone Carvers of Newport, Rhode Island in the 18th Century.* Boston: New England Genealogical Society, 2002.

The Old Burying Ground on the Commons. Photo by Marjory O'Toole.

THE IMPORTANCE OF
UNINSCRIBED STONES

When we visit Little Compton's historic cemeteries, we can't help but be drawn to the carved stones. The grinning skulls, the peaceful angels, the graceful urns or the mysterious hands pointing toward heaven are all fascinating, but to understand the memorialization of most of Little Compton's early residents it is important to look beyond the carved stones to the simple fieldstones standing nearby. There are hundreds of them in the Old Burying Ground on the Commons and many more in the town's family burying grounds.

The vast majority of people buried in Little Compton before the twentieth century were buried with plain fieldstone grave markers or with no markers at all.

- For centuries the Sakonnet People buried their dead without inscribed stones. Even after European settlement and the Christianization of some of the Sakonnets, none were buried with an inscribed stone.

- During the last quarter of the seventeenth century, every Little Compton person of European descent was buried without an inscribed gravestone, at least in part because there were no stone carvers living in the community. Their families could have ordered carved stones from nearby cities, but they chose not to. A handful of families did install backdated, carved stones in the early-eighteenth century, sometimes long after their loved ones' deaths.

- None of Little Compton's approximately 200 enslaved people were buried with carved gravestones either in the Negro Burying Ground on the Commons or in the over forty private burying grounds that dot the landscape.

- No local Baptists chose inscribed stones until the nineteenth century.

- The same is true for the town's Quakers with two exceptions. Elizabeth Taylor was buried with a John Stevens skull-design gravestone in 1714, and Susannah Wilbor's family chose a much simpler Stevens stone with just lettering, no design, in 1729. Then, as Quaker behavioral codes concerning simplicity and ornament tightened, local Friends strictly used uncarved field stones for the next 80 years.

- With only one exception, eighteenth-century children who were stillborn or did not survive long enough to be named were buried without inscribed gravestones. A single, badly-weathered stone reading, "the daughter of Peter and Mary Le Barbie Duplessis born and buried the 2nd day of February 1779," stands in Row 34 of the Old Burying Ground on the Commons.

Photo by Letty Champion.

- From the seventeenth to the early-twentieth century, paupers and strangers buried at the expense of the town had no inscribed gravestones. Many of these people are listed on page 132.

- Only Congregationalists, and only approximately half of them, opted to be buried with carved stones in eighteenth-century Little Compton.

In all of these cases it is important to note that we should say "surviving gravestones." Gravestones do not always survive. There is evidence of Little Compton gravestones breaking or being discarded and of entire burying grounds being destroyed, at times purposely.

Local Congregationalists slowly began using carved gravestones, both headstones and footstones, after the 1700 arrival of stone mason John Stevens. For the next decade, Little Compton's Congregationalists ordered just one or two stones per year. An epidemic in 1711/12 increased the demand for carved gravestones. After that time, about 20 sets of gravestones carved by John Stevens and the other workers at his shop were installed in Little Compton annually for the next several decades.

A 1725 list of sixty-five donors to the Congregational Church helps us understand their use of carved gravestones. If we assume that one's level of giving corresponds at least roughly to one's level of wealth and then check to see which donors were eventually buried with carved gravestones, we learn:

- Only 54% of the donors have a surviving inscribed gravestone in Little Compton or the surrounding communities.

- The least wealthy Congregationalists almost never used inscribed stones.

- Even among the wealthiest eighteenth-century Congregationalists, 30% have no surviving inscribed gravestones.

In early Little Compton carved gravestones were a luxury item, perhaps even a vanity item, that most residents – Native Americans, Africans and African Americans, Quakers, Baptists, paupers, unnamed children and a significant percentage of Congregationalists – either did not choose or were not given.

Instead they were buried with simple fieldstones, one at their head and one at their feet. The distance between the stones indicated the size and therefore, roughly, the age of the person buried. While the footstones in many family lots have survived, those in the Old Burying Ground on the Commons were removed decades ago to make mowing easier, thus eliminating the only indication of whether the buried person was an adult or a child. The use of fieldstones as grave markers, or the use of no marker at all, continued on a small scale in Little Compton well into the twentieth century, especially for those buried at town expense or stillborn children.

As engaging as carved gravestones continue to be, even three hundred years after their making, it is important to remember that they memorialize only a minority of local people. We must not allow them to speak to us too loudly. To do so would neglect the silence of the fieldstones and unmarked graves nearby and the less obvious histories of the hundreds of people they represent.

In a very few cases we can discern who is buried under a specific fieldstone.

At first glance Elisha Clap appears to be buried with a simple fieldstone, but upon close inspection we see that someone, perhaps a family member, perhaps itinerant carver Peter Barker, lightly carved into his stone identifying Elisha and his parents.

Elisha Clap. Photo by Marjory O'Toole.

Sarah Simons' parents buried her with a beautifully carved gravestone, but, unlike any other stone in the burying ground, the Simons used it to alert us to the burial of two unnamed sons buried with simple fieldstones.

> Here lyeth ye body of Sarah,
> ye daughter of William and
> Abigail Simons,
> aged three months and her two brothers,
> one on ye right hand and ye other
> on the left.

In other cases, we can guess what family an uninscribed stone may belong to. This is fairly easy in the town's many family burying grounds, but it is also possible in the Old Burying Ground on the Commons because

Sarah Simons and her brothers. Photo by Marjory O'Toole.

families tended to bury their loved ones together. The Hilliard family is a good example. The Hilliards have numerous carved gravestones in the row closest to the Congregational Church and no family burial ground that we know of. There are uninscribed stones next to Hilliards' carved gravestones. These uninscribed stones likely mark the graves of the older generations of the Hilliard family.

The Bones (also Boen or Bowen) are a more recent example. Charles and Isabella Bone memorialized their four deceased children with two beautifully carved stones dated 1875, 1876, 1891 and 1903. Years later when Charles and Isabella died, Hicks and Potter Funeral Home buried them in the Old Burying Ground at the Commons. It is reasonable to assume they were buried near their children though there are no inscribed stones for the adult Bones or fieldstone markers near the family monument. Ground penetrating radar recently showed the presence of unmarked graves in that area of the cemetery. Two of them may belong to the Bones.

Most of the time, however, it is impossible to match a specific fieldstone with a specific person. The Town of Little Compton did not keep a diagram or any other records noting the specific location of graves in the Old Burying Ground. A newspaper story from the 1870s reports the gravedigger's surprise when he came across a leaded coffin in a part of the Old Burying Ground that was supposed to be empty. The story goes on to say that the gravedigger consulted with the town elders – not town records – all of whom were surprised the coffin was where it was.

Town Council Records did record the names and year of death for many of the people buried at town expense in the Old Burying Ground or in a not-yet-located cemetery at the Town Farm (poor house) on Grange Avenue. Records for 1715/16 allowed for the funeral expenses of John Ryder, a poor laborer whose few belongings were divided between Simon Rouse's tavern and the house of John Price. The Council paid for rum and sugar to be served following the burial, most likely at the tavern, but the town never paid for an inscribed gravestone.

Several newspaper stories about bodies washing up on shore provide us with a few more examples of people buried on the Commons without inscribed gravestones. Most were unidentified, but one was named as part of a sensational mutiny and murder that took place off the Little Compton coast. John Johnson is buried somewhere in the Old Burying Ground on the Commons. Here is his story:

Newspapers up and down the eastern seaboard had a field day in 1843 with stories relating to the "Piracy and Murder" on board the schooner *Sarah Lavinia*. Three crew members murdered their captain and first mate and threw the bodies overboard. They continued sailing for five days, tricking the ship's cook John Johnston into thinking the captain and first mate had fallen overboard in an argument. When they neared Cuttyhunk the two men attacked John Johnston from behind with a mallet and threw him overboard as well. They ransacked the ship, stealing what they could and then scuttled it. They took a small boat to West Island and asked for and received shelter for the night, telling the innkeeper they were headed to New York. When the crew of a passing ship discovered the crime and word spread, the West Island innkeeper, who was not named in the papers, followed the murderers to Providence and found their luggage filled with blood-soaked clothing in the baggage room of the steamship *Massachusetts*. The innkeeper went with law enforcement to New York and successfully identified and captured two of the murderers. Six weeks later a body believed to be John Johnston was found floating on the Sakonnet River and was brought to Little Compton. The body wore sailor's clothing but was in such a poor state that Little Compton's coroner Otis Wilbor could not determine the cause of death nor "whether the deceased was colored or not." Many ship's cooks were African American men. He was "decently interred in the Public Burying Ground in Little Compton."

A partial list of people buried in Little Compton without inscribed gravestones.

A review of Little Compton's records through 1930 has revealed these names of some of the people laid to rest in Little Compton with unmarked graves, uninscribed stones or gravestones that have been lost. Without inscribed gravestones, people can be forgotten from local history. Naming them here is a way to honor their memories and remember them as part of our community.

OBGC = Old Burying Ground on the Commons

Name	Birth	Death	Notes
John Ryder		1716	Buried at Town expense.
Hope Grinell	1699	1752	Buried at Town expense.
John Grinell	1711	1755	Buried at Town expense.
Unnamed "Indeons"		1756	At least five people buried at Town expense.
Mary Slone		1769	Buried at Town expense.
Abigail Gibbs		1771	Buried at Town expense.
John Salsbury		1771	Buried at Town expense.
Isaac Southworth		1773	Buried at Town expense.
Susannah Southworth		1774	Buried at Town expense.

Darker (Dorcas) Suckanush		1774	Buried at Town expense.
Benjamin Brownell		1785	Overseer of the Poor disposes of his property.
Richard Church		1785	Buried at Town expense.
Elizabeth Crandall		1790	Buried at Town expense.
Benjamin Brownell		1790	Buried at Town expense.
Sarah Davenport	1760	1793	Buried at Town expense.
Hannah Wilbour		1793	Buried at Town expense.
Mary Simmons		1795	Buried at Town expense.
Amy Briggs	1790	1796	Buried at Town expense.
Lovet Head's Child		1801	Buried at Town expense.
Elizabeth Brownell		1803	Buried at Town expense.
Expy Sampson		1807	Buried at Town expense.
Adult Female Simmons		1826	Lived at Town Farm. Buried at Town expense.
Ruth Davis		1830	Buried at Town expense.
William Richmond		1833	Buried at Town expense.
Margaret Wilbore		1835	Lived at Town Farm. Buried at Town expense.
Unidentified Male		1839	Buried at Town expense. Washed ashore with dog.
Baby Girl Dring	1841	1841	Daughter of Thomas Dring
John Johnson		1843	Buried in OBGC. Murdered at sea.
Wilbor Brownell	1787	1849	Lived at Town Farm.
Fallee Davis	1775	1849	Lived at Town Farm 12 years.
John Brown	1767	1850	Lived at Town Farm.
Warren Brown	1806	1851	Lived at Town Farm.
John Gifford	1782	1859	"Pauper"
Samuel T. Grennell	1775	1859	"Pauper"
Polly Clapp	1782	1862	Lived at Town Farm 10+ years.
William Salsbury	1787	1862	Lived at Town Farm 20+ years.
Thomas Eldridge	1793	1870	Lived at Town Farm 20+ years.
Lawton Brown	1791	1871	Lived at Town Farm.
Clarissa Chase	1791	1871	Buried at Town expense.
Otis Coggeshall	1794	1872	Lived at Town Farm.
Isaac Clapp	1824	1874	Lived at Town Farm 20+ years.
Anne Marie Sullivan	1871	1874	Ate nightshade.

Mrs. Rathburn		1876	Lived at Town Farm.
Betsey Giffords		1877	Buried at Town expense.
Unknown Person		1879	Buried at Town expense.
John Palmer	1805	1880	Lived at Town Farm.
Unknown Person		1880	Buried at Town expense.
Benjamin Clapp		1883	Buried at Town expense.
Mary Manchester	1805	1883	Lived at Town Farm 15+ years
Unknown Person		1883	Buried at Town expense.
Luther Wilbore	1827	1885	Suicide.
Mira Davoll	1834	1887	Buried at Town expense.
Bertha Manton	1884	1890	Accidental fire.
Alfred Brownell	1809	1891	"Pauper"
Richard Lister	1812	1897	"Pauper"
Theodore Grenell	1841	1903	Resident of Town Farm.
Edward Herenden	1843	1903	"Pauper"
Edward Crowley		1905	Buried in OBGC. Said to have jumped overboard.
Henry Hart	1834	1905	Buried in OBGC.
Sarah Davoll		1906	Buried at Town expense.
James Franklin Kaye	1906	1906	Buried in house yard. Three days old.
Henry Silveira	1906	1906	Buried in OBGC. Premature birth.
Baby Girl Winslow	1907	1907	Two days old.
Baby Girl Sousa	1907	1907	Stillborn.
Baby Oakes	1908	1908	Buried in OBGC.
Baby Girl Almy	1909	1909	Four hours old.
George H. Case	1909	1909	Buried in Family Lot.
Josephine Duwarte	1909	1909	Buried in OBGC. Three months old.
Baby Girl Winslow	1909	1909	Buried at Home. Stillborn
Baby Girl DeSouza	1910	1910	Buried in Home Cemetery. Stillborn.
Albert C.G. Pierce	1845	1911	Buried in Adamsville Cemetery at Town expense.
Baby Boy Kelly	1911	1911	Buried in Family Cemetery. Stillborn.
Deborah Pierce	1836	1911	Buried in Pierce Farm Lot.
Lily Shannon Nickerson	1877	1911	Buried in OBGC. Drowned at sea.

Baby Boy Gomes	1911	1911	Buried at Home. Microencephaly.
Baby Boy Taylor	1911	1911	Buried in lot on Farm. Stillborn.
Olive May Mercer	1909	1912	Buried in OBGC. Three years old.
Baby Boy McDonnell	1916	1916	Buried in Family Cemetery. Stillborn.
Baby Boy Mersey	1917	1917	Buried at Town Farm. Three days old.
Unknown Adult Male		1918	Buried in OBGC. Body found at South Shore Beach
John Lewis	1919	1919	Buried in OBGC. Stillborn.
Unidentified Adult Male		1920	Buried in OBGC. Drowned.
Baby Boy Grazia	1921	1921	Buried in OBGC. Stillborn.
Baby Boy Mello	1921	1921	Buried in OBGC. Stillborn.
Margaret Power	1922	1922	Buried in OBGC. One month old.
Samuel Power	1922	1922	Buried in OBGC. One month old.
Isabel Bennet	1923	1923	Buried in Union Cemetery. Stillborn.
Evelyn May Wordell	1923	1923	Buried in Union Cemetery. Stillborn.
George Henry Case	1928	1928	Buried in Family Lot.
Shirley Gray	1928	1928	Buried in Union Cemetery. Eight months old.
Baby Girl Unknown	1930	1930	Purposely drowned in brook near Main Road. Buried in OBGC.

Photo by Marjory O'Toole.

Professor Jon Marcoux uses ground penetrating radar at the Woodman Lot East. Photo by Marjory O'Toole.

GROUND PENETRATING RADAR

Ground penetrating radar (GPR) is a non-invasive technique used by archeologists to map buried archaeological features. It is especially useful in cemeteries because it does not require any digging.

GPR accurately detects underground objects and features by sending radar waves through the soil and measuring the time it takes for each wave to reflect back to an antenna at the surface. By measuring changes in the speed of the radar waves, GPR can detect the difference between grave shafts and undisturbed ground as well as the presence of buried objects, including caskets, human remains and burial vaults. An analyst can use GPR readings to record both the horizontal position of features as well as their depth below ground, thus

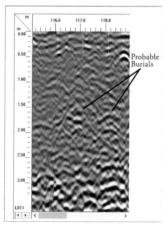

The arch indicates a burial at about six feet.

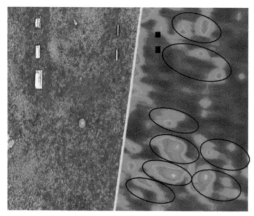

The highly colored areas indicate burials.

The finished map of the Woodman Lot East indicates the possibility of numerous burials in a portion of the burying ground that does not have any gravestones.

RHODE ISLAND
COUNCIL for the HUMANITIES

creating a three-dimensional picture of buried features.

In the spring of 2018, archaeologist Dr. Jon Marcoux, Assistant Professor in the Cultural and Historic Preservation Program at Salve Regina University, shared his GPR expertise with us and surveyed five local cemeteries: a portion of the Old Burying Ground on the Commons that was once the Negro Burying Ground, the Quaker Burying Ground, the Thomas Brownell Burying Ground on Long Highway, and the two Woodman Lots on West Main Road. The results are listed in each cemetery's section in this guide book.

In each case Professor Marcoux created a grid for the cemetery and took radar readings in a regular pattern. The presence of human remains and/or caskets appeared as an arch on the display screen. Dr. Marcoux then flew a drone to capture bird's eye images of each cemetery and superimposed the GPR results on those images to map the location of burials in each cemetery.

His work revealed the presence of numerous unmarked graves and has greatly improved our understanding of our local cemeteries.

This portion of the *Remember Me* project was generously sponsored by the Rhode Island Council for the Humanities, a state affiliate of the National Endowment for the Humanities.

Remember Me